Motorbooks International Illustrated Buyer's Guide Series

Illustrated

CHRYSLER

BUYER'S ★ GUIDE™

D0985672

Richard M. Langworth

Dedicated to the Memory of
Michael P. Langworth, 1907-1995

First published in 1996 by Motorbooks International Publishers & Wholesalers, 729 Prospect Avenue, PO Box 1, Osceola, WI 54020-0001 USA

© Richard M. Langworth , 1996

Motorbooks International books are also available at discounts in bulk quantity for industrial or sales-promotional use. For details write to Special Sales Manager at the Publisher's address

Library of Congress Cataloging-in-Publication Data

Langworth, Richard M.
    Illustrated Chrysler buyer's guide/Richard M. Langworth.
      p. cm.
    Includes index.
    ISBN 0-7603-0106-9 (pbk.: alk.paper)
    1. Chrysler automobile—Purchasing. 2. Chrysler automobile—History. I. Title.
TL215.C55L364   1996
629.222′2—dc20   96-6485

On the front cover: A 1947 Town & Country convertible and a 1960 300F: two of the most collectible cars Chrysler ever produced. *Dave Gooley*

On the back cover: Imperials from two different decades: the hefty 1954 Crown Imperial and the Exner-designed 1961 Imperial convertible. *Author collection*

Printed and bound in the United States of America

Contents

Acknowledgments

I should like to thank Will Fox of *Collectible Automobile* for his diligent work in locating some of the photos herein which I did not have in my own collection, and which were indispensable for the comprehensive illustrations on which the Buyer's Guide series relies. I also thank Jane Mausser, the editorial staff of Motorbooks International, and the countless Chrysler and Imperial owners, drivers, and collectors who provided information or experiences from which to draw upon. I am particularly grateful for the enthusiasm (and continued receipt of publications from) the Chrysler 300 Owners Club. I acknowledge the *Old Cars Value Guide* for prices of most "condition 1" cars in the price history sections, and the *CPI Price Guide* for value ranges on the more recent models.

Finally, I recall again with grateful thanks the comments of many of those on the Dodge scene when some of these cars were new, including the late Virgil Exner, the late Ray Dietrich, the late Murray Baldwin, the late Herb Weissinger, and the very much alive Jeff Godshall, who read and corrected my manuscript, whose distinguished career at Chrysler Design makes him a maker as well as a writer of automotive history, one of the few to do both, and to do both well. Don Narus has been unfailingly helpful over the years on matters relating to the original Town & Country. Don Butler and Bill Tilden, both students of Chrysler history, were similarly helpful in the broader sense. The late Jim Bradley, former curator of the Automotive History Collection, Detroit Public Library, was a mentor and friend whose encouragement was crucial to my auto writing career. Lee Iacocca, who took the time from a hectic schedule to write the occasional letter of encouragement, was not crucial, but respectfully appreciated.

Introduction

My Roadmaster bike had a car badge wired to its huge, dual front springs and the South Jersey neighbor kid spotted it. The badge was from a set of flashy round metal car emblems you found in boxes of Wheaties, Cheerios and Kix.

"What kind of a car does *your dad* drive?" he said waspishly.

"Chrysler," I said, guessing what was coming.

"I knew it! You New York City kids don't think for yourselves at all. If your dad drove a Crosley [he named the American marque most likely to be recognized as beneath contempt in 1952] you'd have a Crosley emblem on your bike."

It was a tough accusation. My father *did* own a Chrysler, and I wouldn't have thought of putting any other Cheerios car badge on my Roadmaster.

The car in question was a 1952 Chrysler Windsor Deluxe four-door sedan. It was a used car in the technical sense, meaning that Dad bought it in 1953 with 10,000 miles on the odometer, trading in his old '49 Dodge Meadowbrook. The Windsor was metallic green with deep green velour upholstery immediately protected—I could never figure out what we were protecting it from—by slipcovers, the habit of the time. It had a jukebox-style instrument binnacle clustered under an immense steering wheel; a rock-hard vinyl "crash pad" across the rest of the dash, a heater with big chrome knobs that looked like bathtub taps, and a six-tube radio producing wonderful fat sounds, with a little window in the dial that went from "Speech" to "Mello" as you adjusted the tone control.

My father was a confirmed believer in Chrysler products. Before the Dodge he'd owned a '38 Plymouth. He had moved up, step by step, from the company's least expensive make to a middle priced and then a near-luxury product, just as Walter Percy Chrysler had planned when building his automotive empire in the image of Alfred Sloan's General Motors.

Dad had every reason to believe that a Chrysler meant he had arrived. He was celebrating five years of success in the florist business on Staten Island, New York. He'd *earned* this big Windsor, sweated for it with my mother, handling a finicky clientele

for 300 six-day, sixty-hour weeks since 1949. The Windsor was slow and thirsty and looked like it had been designed by the Erector Set inventor; but it was a wonderful, soul-filling luxury chariot that rode like a dream and was simply impervious to harm. The doors chunked shut like a refrigerator's and the hood and deck clanged down like manhole covers. If you ran into it with a Volkswagen, you'd have to take it to a body shop and have the Bug taken out.

Years later I still carried a figurative Chrysler badge engraved on my brain, still nurturing (and having driven) Plymouths, Dodges, DeSotos, Chryslers, and Imperials. Virgil Exner, Chrysler's chief of design from 1951 to 1961, was as heroic to me as Robert E. Lee and Winston Churchill. The first book I wrote was on Kaiser-Frazer, a temporary and inexplicable lapse. The second book I wrote was about Chrysler and Imperial, and many books and articles on the same followed. It is appropriate now that the last automotive book I am likely to write is on the same subject, for Chrysler Corporation (thanks to Lee Iacocca) is just as interesting now as it was when I was challenged by a fellow bicyclist in 1953.

I have had the fortune to be an automotive writer at what, in my increasing dotage, I view ever more strongly as the "golden age" of car collecting, the mid-sixties to the mid-eighties. In those years we could all afford an old car, or three or four of them. In 1970, when I joined the staff of *Automobile Quarterly*, the only "marque history" of a domestic make was Bob Turnquist's *The Packard Story*; the field was wide open, and I had the pleasure of writing my share of books, editing and contributing to others. To borrow a phrase from Dean Acheson, I was "Present at the Creation." I learned a great deal and was able to make a lot of valuable contacts. I soon fulfilled my childhood Chrysler fantasies by meeting and interviewing Virgil Exner and some of his lieutenants. I became hooked on the story of Exner's years at Chrysler, how he took a company renowned for the dowdy plainness of its styling and gave it products which were the envy of the design profession by 1956 (the year of the "Forward Look") and 1957 (the year of "Flight Sweep").

Chrysler-Plymouth is the only survivor from the corporate structure of the 1930s through 1950s, still intact from the time when Walter Chrysler set out to mimic General Motors with a compartmentalized corporate structure meshed to a pecking order which the typical customer would mount, a step at a time. Beginning 1930 there was a Dodge, DeSoto, and Plymouth Division as well as Chrysler, with each dealership getting Plymouth, for volume, along with one of the other three. The idea was that you'd start with a Plymouth, then trade for a Dodge, DeSoto, and finally a Chrysler as your worldly goods accumulated.

For thirty years this worked just fine, but in 1960 following a disastrous recession, DeSoto was blended into Plymouth-Valiant Division, and then vanished forever; Dodge soldiered on all by itself; and Chrysler and Plymouth Divisions were merged, but their dealers kept their "Chrysler-Plymouth" signs. Unfortunately, the separate-make Imperial melded back into Chrysler in the 1970s, and has reappeared only fitfully to date. Chrysler did retain a distinct identity as a near-luxury car and, since the last departure of Imperial, a full-luxury car. For years Chrysler assured the public it would never build a small car; when that position became inevitable in the mid-seventies, it nevertheless built *luxurious* small cars. This faithfulness to its image has attracted fans to the Chrysler marque over the years. Vast numbers of old Chryslers have survived, to be restored lovingly by a new generation who never knew the cars when new. The aim of this book is to codify and categorize the collectible Chrysler and Imperial for that new generation of car collectors.

This Buyer's Guide covers every Chrysler and Imperial built from 1924 through the early 1970s, and collectible (or potentially collectible) Chryslers from the mid-1970s to the present. It is, of course, impossible to predict now how a car as new as the Sebring LXi will be viewed by the collector crowd twenty or thirty years hence, but you can get a rough idea by going out and driving one. It's a nice thing that in an age of jellybean-shaped transportation modules, some companies with distinguished names are still building automobiles to excite the senses— cars which stand to be remembered long after their time.

Each chapter adheres to the following format:

History: a background, placing the models covered in historical perspective, and noting their success or failure at the time.

Identification: how to tell one model from another, and features of various model years.

Appraisal: comparative considerations of all the cars in each chapter as to their collectibility versus each other (and other contemporary, similar makes), and the perils or joys of ownership.

Summary and prospects: current collectibility and/or prospects for changes in this status.

Price History: a thirteen-year comparison of top values for near-perfect show-quality examples of various cars under discussion.

Production: model year figures for the various models, sub-models, and body styles under discussion.

Specifications: basic engine, chassis, and drivetrain figures, along with wheelbases, weights, tire sizes, and typical performance figures. I have not troubled to provide incredibly detailed specs because they are so readily available elsewhere; to that end I recommend the comprehensive *Standard Catalogs of American Cars* published by Krause Publications and available through Classic Motorbooks. Three of these (covering 1805-1942, 1946-1975, and 1976-1986, plus a Chrysler derivation of them) are exhaustive and invaluable in laying out reams of data as to specifications, equipment, options, and original prices.

Rereading these chapters and recalling the Chryslers I've driven over the years, from a 1930 Imperial to the 1995 LHS, makes me realize how little Chrysler's role has really changed: a quality car at a reasonable price. I was hooked on the marque when I first cast eyes on my dad's Windsor with its big wide grille and glitzy dash, and I'm still hooked. After nearly fifteen years as a Saab owner, I've made the decision to buy American. The American car has come a long way in that time, and almost certainly my next everyday car will be an LHS: the first Chrysler in more than thirty years that I could seriously see myself enjoying round the clock.

Richard M. Langworth
Hopkinton, New Hampshire

Investment Ratings

★★★★★ **The best Chryslers.**

Rarely advertised, these top-value, blue-chip Chryslers tend to change hands quietly between private parties, mainly through word of mouth or club contacts rather than by commercial advertising, although they are certainly advertised and occasionally sell for high prices at auctions. They represent the top collector Chryslers, with high potential for long-term appreciation. This rating has not been applied to recent models because the values of those models have not yet settled to the point where long-term judgments can be made.

★★★★ **The next-best Chryslers.**

These are usually scarce or even rare models, with low original production runs. They are not easily found, but are constantly sought after by collectors and have a strong investment potential. They include most of the high-roller performance cars and are better short-term investments than the five-star selections. They are found often in hobby advertising, but not so often in newspapers. Auctions feature them prominently. The best sources for these cars are the Chrysler clubs.

★★★ **Excellent values.**

Chryslers in reasonably good supply, though by no means common, that have demonstrated good investment value over the short to middle term, are rated three stars. They are good choices for combination drivers and show cars. They may include "sleepers" that will move up to the higher categories.

★★ **Good values.**

I like to equate these to an off-year Bordeaux: sound, well made, ready to be enjoyed right now, not set aside for future appreciation. All are reasonably priced. They are not appreciating as rapidly as the more highly rated cars, but neither are they losing value. The odds are good that you'll be able to sell one for more than you paid, provided you don't overindulge in restoration work.

★ **Potentially collectible.**

Speculative ventures, including many recent models (which are hard to judge with finality) get one-star ratings. This should not dissuade you if you find an exceptionally clean original model and the price is right. Often these cars are too young to establish a firm state of value but they have certain characteristics of earlier Chryslers that are now highly sought after. In other cases they are cars that have been on the Chryslers scene a long time without moving up much in value.

Price History

A broker can go to jail by claiming specific future performance for a security, but there's nothing wrong with examining where that security has been in the past. Thus I present here the price history of top show-quality cars over the past decade or more, as a means of gauging its likely future behavior on the old car market.

My baseline year for most cars is 1980 because that's as far back as I can find reliable asking prices, auction, and sales information. Along with the 1995 typical price for a 95+ point (near-perfect trophy-winning) example, I have calculated the rate of return, assuming you invested the 1980 price then and sold for the 1995 price today.

Thus, for example, if you bought a 1955 Chrysler 300 in prime condition for, say $8,000 in 1980, and your car is worth $32,000 today, that represents a compound rate of return of 14% on your money, which is better than most mutual funds are paying. (In fact you'll find some 300 "letter series" cars returning much better than that on your money, if you bought them right, and enough years ago . . .)

Cars, of course, are not CDs or stock portfolios; they require maintenance, insurance, parts, and service. Also, the price figures are highly arbitrary, taken from three or four sources and averaged. Prices apply only to very fine, condition 1 original or (more likely) restored cars, which always command far more than the same models in mediocre condition.

It is not possible individually to measure the overhead involved in twelve years' ownership of any specific car. Obviously, running costs are going to be higher for a 1957 300C than they are for a '50 Newportt. On the other hand, the rate of return does not take into consideration the intangible fun of ownership, which, after all, counts for something. Maybe the two balance each other out.

Chapter 1

The Chrysler Six
1924-34

The car which led to Detroit's third great automotive empire was a touring model (then the most popular type) priced at $1,335, $40 more than the Buick 24/45, aimed squarely at the medium price field. Officially the B-series, it was soon joined by a eight other body styles including a "Crown Imperial." An "Imperial" in those days was a body type, but it wasn't long before Chrysler made the term its own, with a long-running model designation that would be around in one form or another for sixty years.

The Chrysler marque sprang from Maxwell-Chalmers, which Walter P. Chrysler, flushed with success at Buick and Willys-Overland, came to lead as chairman of the board in 1921. Maxwell was heading downhill; Chrysler turned it around, bringing with him many ingenious people who would help him build the car and corporation bearing his name.

The first Chrysler was engineered by a close-knit technical triumvirate that has no parallel in automotive history: Fred M. Zeder, Owen Skelton, and Carl Breer. These worthies, who had come from Willys-Overland with Chrysler, were given a clean sheet of paper and a basic specification: a 2,400lb car on a 110in wheelbase which could do 60mph. What they created exceeded the target weight and dimensions slightly, but more importantly exceeded the performance goal by 10mph, and Chrysler named it the Model B70 in honor of its top speed. In prototype form by July 1923, the Chrysler Six was produced under the auspices of another famous Chrysler recruit, George W. Mason, who would come to head Nash in 1936 and found American Motors in 1954. "I am building the Chrysler," said Walter P., "because I have been convinced for years that the public has a definite idea of a real quality light car—not extravagantly large and heavy for one or two people but adequately roomy for five, economical to own and operate."

Although it looked similar to the concurrent Maxwell, the Chrysler's broad chrome plated radiator shell distinguished it, as did its pathfinding specifications. Zeder, Skelton, and Breer had designed the Chrysler Six without regard to cost or compromise, achieving remarkable efficiency, silence, smoothness, and flexibility. It had a one-piece nickel-chrome alloy iron block and a detachable cast-iron cylinder head. Valves were disposed in an L-head arrangement, and the combustion chambers were laid out for high turbulence according to Ricardo principles so that compression could be high without detonation problems. Zeder chose forged steel connecting rods and a chain-driven camshaft; the crankshaft was a massive steel forging with integral counterweights and seven main bearings. Chryslers also had full-pressure lubrication, a replaceable element oil filter, an air cleaner that functioned as a silencer, a Ball updraft carburetor, and Remy coil-and-battery ignition.

As finely machined and engineered as the engine was, the Chrysler's four-wheel Lockheed hydraulic brakes were what really started people talking. As a sales feature they were as important as "ABS" is today, almost unheard of at the time, certainly on a car costing only about $1,400. They completely eclipsed the then-standard mechanical brakes, affording balanced brake force distribution and high reliability. Almost 20,000 Sixes were registered during 1924. An expanded line of 1925 70s racked up close to 70,000 registrations, and in June, Walter Chrysler founded Chrysler Corporation, intent on building a multi-make combine that would take on the industry leaders: Ford, GM, and his old company, Willys-Overland.

The Imperial name was broken out as a separate model designation for the first time in 1926, on a wholly new, longer, and far more luxurious Series E80, named for *its* top speed, produced by an enlarged Chrysler Six.

The Imperial was a bold foray into Cadillac territory, and was even thought to rival some models of Packard, the standard of the day. Chrysler romped into sixth place in the industry that year, when Kaufman Thuma ("K.T.") Keller joined the company as Vice-President; after Walter Chrysler's demise Keller would lead the company into the postwar period.

A new, light, and fast 60 series was introduced for 1927, and the 70 became the "Finer 70,"

The first year for Chrysler is represented here by a B-series touring. Instantly identifiable by its "silver-winged" helmet radiator mascot and massive radiator surround, the new 1924 Chrysler's best features were under the skin: a smooth inline Six and four-wheel Lockheed drum brakes. There were other competitive Sixes, but few rivals except Buick had four-wheel brakes. The touring sold for $1,335; disk wheels were standard, bumpers an accessory. The split windshield with opening lower section was apparently an option, as one-piece windshields are also found. *Publications International Ltd.*

running alongside the continued Imperial. Though powered by a somewhat downsized engine, the new 60 was a sprightly, popular model, and incorporated the four-wheel hydraulic brakes for which Chrysler had become famous. It sold well. Progress continued in 1928, when the Imperial expanded to a 136in wheelbase and Chrysler racked up over 142,000 registrations, its highest until 1950. The Chrysler Four (see next chapter) became the Plymouth in 1929, introduced inauspiciously as the stock market crashed, but six-cylinder cars continued to be Chrysler's mainstay. In 1930 there were four different engines ranging from just under 200 to just over 300ci, and prices spread from $845 to $3,075. The last Imperial Sixes were built this year, but only a relative handful, hardly more than 600: the Depression was on, and all-out luxury cars were slow sellers.

With the corporation acquiring Dodge and bringing out Plymouth and DeSoto in the late twenties, Chrysler management began to target the flagship make at the upper-medium and high priced fields. This did not immediately affect the Chrysler Six, which continued to power new models: the "New Series Six" or model CM in mid-1931, with its rakish v-shaped radiator, wide profile, and double-dropped frame allowing what one writer rather optimistically termed a "Cord L29 look." Nonetheless, Chrysler Sixes were well proportioned and continued to appeal to those who could afford them. The Model 70 that had started it all was continued into 1932, but production ceased by May of that year.

For 1933 Chrysler pared the Six down to just one model, the handsome CO, on a 117in wheelbase; though all other Chryslers were now Eights, the CO cost less and therefore sold most, about 20,000 units for the model year. This was hardly inspiring, but at a time when Ford and Chevy considered 300,000 units pretty good, it was enough to keep the Chrysler make in the top ten. Eclipsed by the Airflow in 1934, the Six appeared in two new, beautifully streamlined models, the

The 1924 Imperial line included this B-series five-passenger sedan, which sold for $1,895, and a more luxurious Crown Imperial priced $300 higher. An Imperial town car was also available. *Publications International Ltd.*

Specifications

Engines (net hp)
Type: cast-iron inline Six, seven main bearings
180ci (3 x 4.25in), 54-60hp:1927-28 60 Series
190ci (3.38 x 4.25in), 65-70hp: 1929 60 Series
196ci (3.38 x 4.5in), 62-65hp: 1930 60 (early), 1931 CJ6
201ci (3 x 4.75in), 68hp: 1924-25 all models
218ci (3.25 x 4.38in), 78hp: 1931-32 CM6 (New Six)
219ci (3.38 x 4.75in), 68hp: 1926-27 G70, 1930-31 66
219ci (3.38 x 4.75in), 75hp: 1930 70 (early)
224ci (3.25 x 4.5in), 82hp: 1932 CI6 ("Second Series")
224ci (3.25 x 4.5in), 84-89hp: 1933 all models
242ci (3.38 x 4.5in), 93-100hp: 1934 all models
249ci (3.25 x 5in), 75-84hp: 1928-29 70 Series
269ci (3.38 x 5in), 93hp: 1930 70 (late), 1931-32 70
288ci (3.5 x 5in), 92hp: 1926-27 E80 Imperial
309ci (3.63 x 5in.), 100-112hp: 1928-30 Imperial

Chassis and Drivetrain
1924-25: Ladder chassis, conventional clutch, shaft drive, four-wheel hydraulic brakes, steel disc wheels on touring, wood-spoke wheels on other models. Three-speed manual transmission with floor shift.
1928: Wood spoke or wire wheels available.
1929-32: Four-speed multi-range manual transmission on all Series except 66, CJ, CM, CI which retained the three-speed.
1933-34: Three-speed manual transmission with floor shift.

Size and Weight
Wheelbase (in):
70 Series, 1924-27: 112.8in; 1928-29: 120.5in; 1930-32: 116.5in
Imperial 80, 1926: 120in; 1927: 120 & 127in; 1928-29: 136in
60 Series, 1927-28: 109in; 1929-31: 113in
CJ Series, 1930-31: 109in
CM ("New Six"), CI ("Second Series"), CO, 1930-33: 116in
CA, 1934: 118in
Curb Weight (lb):
1924-29: 2,500-3,300lb, Imperials: 2,900-3,800lb; 1930-34: 2,600-3,200lb

CA and CB, powered by an enlarged engine with up to 100hp. A handful of open models were built in both series, and these are highly collectible today, though many bystanders think Chrysler was building nothing but Airflows in the mid-thirties. Fortunately, they had something else to offer. The Sixes accounted for about three-quarters of 1934 sales!

Identification

1924: Thick, rounded radiator shell with "Viking helmet" radiator cap sprouting double wings; split windshields on early models; drum headlamps; double beltline molding on closed models.

1925: One piece windshields hinged at the top; extended gearshift lever; Lanchester vibration damper; rubber engine mounts.

1926: higher door openings; bullet headlamps on open models at midyear; long-wheelbase Imperial Series E80 introduced.

1927: Oval instrument panels; new Series 60 introduced; bullet headlamps and scalloped hood/radiator on Imperials.

1928: New rectangular instrument panel with indirect illumination; narrow, high-pitched "cadet" windshield visor on Series 52/62; headlight posts attached to frame on Series 72; early Imperials carried over from 1927; later Imperials on new 136-inch wheelbase.

1929: Narrow profile radiators, key ignition, shallow bowl shaped headlamps, silver and black instrument panel on Series 65, gold and black on 75; arched vertical hood louvers on Imperials.

1930: Narrow profile radiator, bowl shaped headlights, heavier fenders, "pennon" hood louvers (changed to vertical on later 70s and 77s); last year for six-cylinder Imperials.

1931: Series CJ, 66 and 70 carried over from 1930; cowl lamps mounted on a belt molding between hood and cowl (known as "surcingle"); 66 carried headlamp tie-bar with "66" emblem; 70s had a new, low, flat, vee'd radiator.

1932: Series CM and 70 carried over from 1931; Series CI had new oval instrument panel, split-vee windshields on closed cars, dual cowl ventilators, larger hubcaps covering wheel lugs.

1933: Long hood without separate cowl; door type hood ventilators; single windshield wiper; massive front fenders sweeping down almost to bumper height at front; single bar bumpers, vee'd radiator grille.

1934: Only non-Airflows in Chrysler line (Models CA and CB); skirted front fenders; front vent windows; dual windshield wipers; steel spoke wheels; "suicide doors" on all models except CB convertible sedan.

Appraisal

The current value structure of early Chrysler Sixes varies little from year to year. The very finest 90-point restorations (non-Imperials) cost about $20,000-25,000 if they're open body styles, or about $12,000-15,000 if closed. Among the open, there's little difference in value between phaetons and roadsters; among the closed bodies, the longer wheelbase coupes are the most desirable. Imperials are a different matter: the best open examples are the 1929-30 models (the last six-cylinder Imperials), which can cost up to $75,000 for a show-winning restoration with a custom body (typically by Locke). Imperial roadsters and phaetons, factory bodied, top out at around $60,000.

Summary and Prospects

These are fine driving cars, beautifully engineered and styled in the contemporary twenties idiom. Though scarce, they are not high performers as investment items, being for the most part lost in the dead zone of car collecting (1918-1925), eclipsed by their senior eight-cylinder brethren (1931-33) or the Airflow (1934). Early thirties models are particularly good values, being no more expensive than their predecessors but much more up to date with rakish, smooth lines on coupes and convertibles. A number of Imperials wore custom bodies by Fleetwood, Locke, and others; these are commensurably more valuable than factory bodies, especially in open form. Still, overall, a collector car, not an investment.

Return on investment (95-point condition 1):

	1980	1995	Return
1925 B70 sedan	$10,000	$10,000	0
1929 E80 Imperial dual cowl phaeton	$32,000	$75,000	7.5%

*compound annual rate of return unadjusted for maintenance, insurance, and running costs

Production

Prior to 1930, Chrysler production figures are ephemeral and incomplete. I have listed what I could find, including total registrations (not a full gauge of calendar or model year production) and breakdowns of some (but not all) individual models.

A handsome 1930 Series 70 cabriolet for the export market. Domestic 70s had cowl-mounted auxiliary lights although prototypes carried them high in the windshield post. This example shows none, but if intended for Europe they were probably mounted up front with the headlamps. *Publications International Ltd.*

Year	Registrations
1924	19,960
1925	68,793
1926*	44,565
1927	71,822
1928	65,167
1929	84,520

*1926 figure is author's estimate

Series 62/65 known production:

Year	Registrations
1928	64,136
1929	65,472

1928 Series 72 models: 2-4p coupe, 6,869; touring, 32; roadster, 6,416; convertible coupe, 1,729; 4p coupe, 2,378; Crown sedan, 3,266; LeBaron town cabriolet, 36; close-coupled and town sedan, 4,977.

1928 Imperial models: 7p sedan, 374; 7p limousine, 86; sedan, 790; roadster, 281. *Dietrich* models: convertible sedan, 10; dual-cowl phaeton, 6; 7p phaeton, 5; sedan, 4. *LeBaron* models: convertible coupe, 39; dual-cowl phaeton, 31; town coupe, 21; close-coupled sedan, 4; 5p coupe, 3; 7p town sedan, 1. *Derham* models: convertible sedan, 1.

1929 Series 65 models: sedan, 24,958; coach, 8,846; 4p coupe, 7,603; roadster, 4,953; 2p coupe, 4,655; phaeton, 248; sport touring, 71.

1929 Series 75 models: Royal sedan, 22,456; 2p coupe, 9,488; roadster, 6,414; town sedan, 3,408; convertible coupe, 1,430; 4p coupe, 1,016; convertible sedan, 337; tonneau phaeton, 227; phaeton, 11.

1929 Imperials: 5p sedan, 838; 7p sedan, 442; town sedan, 379; 7p limousine, 99. *Locke* models: roadster, 401 (1929-30 combined); convertible coupe, 142; sport phaeton, 41; 7p phaeton, 15. *LeBaron* models: 2-4p coupe, 149.

	1930-31 CJ6 (wb 109.0")	1930-31 66 (wb 112.8")	1930-31 70 (wb116.5")
roadster, 2-4p	1,616	1,213	1,431
phaeton, 5p	0	26	279
touring, 5p	279	0	0
business coupe	2,267	2,014	766
Royal coupe, 2-4p	3,593	3,257	3,135
Royal sedan	20,748	3,753	11,213
brougham, 5p	0	2,343	1,204
convertible coupe	705	0	705
chassis	31	0	0

	1930-31 77 (wb 124.0")	1930 Imperial (wb 136.0")
roadster, 2-4p	1,729	*100
phaeton	173 (5p)	*15 (7p)
business coupe	230	
Royal coupe, 2-4p	2,954	
Crown coupe, 2-4p	883	
convertible coupe	418	*50
Royal sedan	7,211	
Town sedan	436	*100
Crown sedan	2,654	
sedan, 5p	0	*300
sedan, 7p	0	*150

* estimates by author

	1931-32 CM6 (wb 116.0")	1932 CI (wb 116.0)
roadster, 2-4p	2,281	474
coupe	5,327	2,913
sedan	28,6201	3,772
phaeton	196	59
business coupe	802	354
convertible coupe	1,492	1,000
convertible sedan	0	322
chassis	997	0

	1933 CO (wb 117.0")	1934 CA (wb 118.0")	1934 CB (wb 118.0")
business coupe	587	1,650	0
coupe	1,454	1,875	0
convertible coupe	677	700	0
brougham	1,207	1,575	0
sedan	13,264	17,617	980
sedan, 7p	202	0	0
convertible sedan	205	0	450
chassis	267	385	20

Chapter 2

The Chrysler Four
1926-28

Walter P. Chrysler built his corporation from Maxwell-Chalmers, and when his first Chrysler was introduced, he was still building four-cylinder Maxwells. Resurrecting that make from a recent slough of reliability problems, he offered free repairs in the field; in 1924 he brought out an improved Maxwell, but once the Chrysler brand was established he dropped Maxwell and launched the Chrysler Four. This model was really not what W.P. had in mind for the car bearing his name, and in mid-1928 he brought out a Ford/Chevy rival to replace the four-cylinder Chrysler. What to call it was a question, but Joe Frazer, his sales vice president, solved that by coming up with the patriotic moniker of Plymouth. "Boss," said Frazer, "you must have heard of Plymouth Binder Twine," referring to a popular agricultural product. "Hell, Joe, every goddamn farmer in America's heard of that," said the boss, and the Plymouth had arrived.

The shortlived Chrysler Four was therefore a Maxwell in all but name, introduced in 1926 under the Chrysler "58" label. It wasn't a bad car; it wasn't a real Chrysler either, but the latter brand had not been around long enough to worry over any preconceived market niches. Priced at around $1,000, lower than the previous Maxwell, the Model 58 was a good buy for the money, offered in five body styles: coach (club sedan), four-door sedan, coupe, touring, and roadster. Bodies were built by Budd in Philadelphia; a family resemblance to the big Chrysler was retained through the rounded radiator shell with "Viking helmet" mascot, beltline moldings, and "cadet" visors on closed body styles.

For 1927 the Four was called "Series 50," had a shorter wheelbase but three additional models: rumble seat roadster, leather trimmed sedan, and landau sedan with dummy landau bars. The 1928 model was a continuation of this series, now called the 52.

Identification

1926: The 109in wheelbase, later used on junior Sixes, was the shortest yet found on a Chrysler.

One-piece windshield on closed cars, two-piece on open. Drum-type headlamps. Instruments and controls in an oval dashboard panel.

1927: Like 1926, but wheelbase reduced to 106in.

1928: Bullet-shaped headlamps and, on closed body styles, a narrower, more sharply pitched visor. Indirect instrument panel illumination was provided for the first time; gauges and controls were housed in a rectangular panel. The 106in wheelbase was retained. One-piece windshield on all models except touring.

Appraisal

Lacking the get-up-and-go of the Chrysler Six, these little Fours were nevertheless beautifully built with all the precision of their senior counterparts, and the Budd bodies were solid. In collector

Strictly a stopgap, the last four-cylinder Chrysler for over fifty years was brought out in 1926 as the Model 58; essentially it was the old Maxwell, a marque which had been dropped after Chrysler took over that company. The 1926 models ride a 109in wheelbase; this was reduced to 106in in 1927-28. The coupe was the least expensive closed model; like the coach and sedan, it carried a one-piece windshield and "cadet" visor. *Publications International Ltd.*

of that in "restorable" shape; only coupe models are capable of breaking five figures.

Summary and Prospects

Antique cars have for years been the slowest moving in terms of value appreciation, and many antique car collectors say this is just fine with them: they're not in it for the money, and they prefer to buy and sell their cars at pre-inflation levels. The odds are overwhelming that these will remain strictly cars for the Chrysler enthusiast, not the speculator.

Return on investment (95-point condition 1):

	1980	**1995**	***Return**
1928 Series 52 rumble seat roadster	$13,000	$22,000	4.2%
1928 Series 52 sedan	$6,000	$7,500	1.7%

*compound annual rate of return unadjusted for maintenance, insurance, and running costs

car parlance, all were built before 1930 and are therefore strictly "antiques." Still, this is one of the few Chrysler models for which you can buy a 90-point open body for less than $20,000: only the rumble seat roadster tends to break that barrier. Closed models, on the other hand, cost under $10,000 in prime condition and barely ten percent

Production

1926	1927	1928
*85,000	82,412	76,857

* author's estimate

The most common open Chrysler Four was the touring, priced at $2,390. Note the two-piece windshield, common to this and the roadster model. Belt-line moldings and radiator shape with winged ornament duplicated hallmarks of the larger Chryslers. *Publications International Ltd.*

★★★★★	Imperial
★★★	Others

The Chrysler Eight
1931-33

Chrysler's 1931 model plans were largely determined by the sales performance of its '29 models. Although the concept of a "model year" beginning each autumn had yet to be adopted widely, Chrysler's run of each year's models began well in advance of the calendar year. Thus the '31s had to be locked up no later than very early 1930. This explains why Chrysler launched a more expensive straight eight just as the Depression rang down the lid on luxury car sales.

By 1929 both K.T. Keller and Walter P. Chrysler believed the straight eight would dominate Chrysler's upper-medium price field. To free production capacity for Eights, Keller slashed the number of Sixes, not only for Chrysler but for Dodge and DeSoto as well. Chrysler, being the most expensive of these makes, actually received four different Eights, ranging from a 240ci unit for the 1931 "New Eight" (built late 1930) to a mighty 385 for the 1931 Imperial. The latter really reached its pinnacle in 1931-33. These were the Imperials of style and splendor, every one of which is rated a true "Classic" by the Classic Car Club of America.

The Imperial Eight was a smooth, low-revving L-head with nine main bearings, capable of propelling these nearly 5,000lb cars up to 100mph and from 0 to 60 in 20 seconds, a singular feat six decades ago. Equally distinguished was their styling, the product of Chrysler's first design studio under a talented young man named Herb Weissinger, who would later win fame at Kaiser-Frazer. He was chiefly responsible for the long, low bodies on Imperial's enormous 145in wheelbase, the gracefully curved fenders and a rakish grille strongly resembling that of the Cord L-29. Imperials were available in a plethora of glorious open bodies by Chrysler (via Briggs), LeBaron (semi-custom), and the following full-custom body builders: Waterhouse, Locke, Derham, and Murphy. Open models comprised roadsters, sport phaetons, convertible coupe, and convertible sedan. Remarkably, only the convertible sedan sold for more than $3,600. They were incredible bargains—but in 1931 few people had the money, and those who had it did not want to flaunt it.

Production was minuscule, a few hundred of each body type at best.

The smaller Chrysler Eights on wheelbases around 125in were also beautifully proportioned and produced in rather larger quantities. The first of these was the 1931 Series CD, which was replaced in May 1931 by a Deluxe CD. In 1932 a line of 135in wheelbase Imperials was introduced, but the following year Chrysler downsized drastically, bringing out a small line of Eights called Royals on 120in and running the smaller Imperials on 126in with a smaller engine. All these fine cars were eclipsed in 1934 by the Chrysler Airflow, and whatever people said about that, they agreed on at least one thing: it wasn't the same.

Identification

1931: Wide profile V-type radiator similar to the L-29 Cord, twin cowl vents, vertical louver hoods, sloping windshield. Deluxe CD has split windshield, screened V-type radiator.

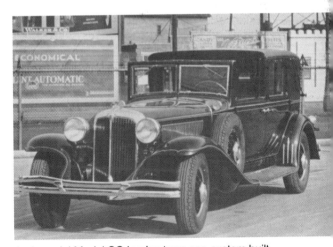

An Imperial Model CG landau town car, custom built on the long, 145in wheelbase and powered by Chrysler's largest Eight, was an impressive conveyance for the carriage trade in 1931. Unique split windshield was a feature exclusive to the Imperial and Deluxe Eight. *Publications International Ltd.*

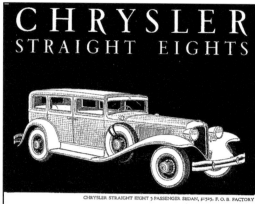

Although market trends in the late twenties moved manufacturers toward more cylinders, Walter Chrysler had always wanted to build an Eight. Half a century and more after it first appeared, the 1931-33 Eight stands as a high point in Chrysler history, and these cars are the most expensive and desirable Chryslers. Emphasizing the flexibility of its "dual high gears" is this ad from February 1931. *Publications International Ltd.*

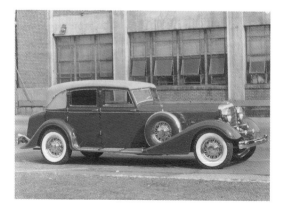

1932: Deluxe Eight Series CD and Imperial CG Series carried over unchanged into early 1932. Second Series CP Eight (mid-model year) featured all-steel bodies, new double drop frame, narrow Vee'd radiator, split V-type windshields on closed cars and an optional automatic vacuum clutch. New smaller Imperial CH Series on 135-inch wheelbase; the larger Imperial continued as the CL Series and can be distinguished from the CH by its walnut dashboard and engine-turned metal panel for the instruments.

1933: Chrysler adopted the model year concept this year, which made matters less confusing, and the Chrysler Eight came in three models: the short wheelbase Royal, the baseline Imperial, and the Imperial Custom, the latter still riding a 12ft-plus wheelbase but down to only a handful of cars. Royals had single bar bumpers, "suicide" doors, sloping v-shaped radiator, slanting windshield, door type hood vents. Base Imperials (Series CQ) were on a smaller 126in wheelbase and had similar styling, but "suicide" doors only on the convertible coupe. Custom Imperials (Series CL) had a full-length hood with no cowl and "suicide" doors on all models except the limousine. Semi-custom LeBaron bodies were still catalogued but only six chassis were supplied for full-custom work, two of which went, curiously, to Lagenthawl and Oygas in Geneva.

Appraisal

Values of Chryslers in this period can be grouped by wheelbase. The 1931-32 Eights and 1933 Imperial (all around 125in) command about $30,000 for a show-winning open example and half that for closed bodies. The big 145/146in Imperials are much more valuable, bringing as much as $350,000 for custom-bodied open models and not much less for LeBaron and Briggs (Chrysler) semi-customs. Properly restored, an Imperial coupe can top $100,000. The mid-range Series CH 1932 Imperials, which did not include custom bodies, sell for $40,000 (sedan), $60,000 (coupe), and over $200,000 (convertible sedan). Bear in mind that these prices are all for top quality restorations; an unrestored Imperial, or old restoration in need of complete reworking, can be

Left
Walter Percy Chrysler's personal car, a LeBaron bodied Imperial sedan-limousine built in late 1932 on the 146in Series CL chassis. Special features include fabric covered top with dummy landau bars, dual air horns, and early-style bowl shaped headlamps: a fabulous car, redolent of the extremes of custom coachcraft on the Imperial chassis. *Publications International Ltd.*

A 1931 Deluxe Eight convertible, export issue, at a rally of the Classic American Auto Club of Great Britain at Blenheim Palace in 1977. A small number of Eights have survived in Europe, though nowadays the demand has most of them being shipped east to west.

acquired for $40,000 for open customs, if you can find one—that's the main problem because most of the existing examples are in restored condition. The 1933 Royal on its shorter wheelbase commands $30,000 for the finest open models and as little as $12,000 for a four-door sedan or brougham. Taken as a group, the long-wheelbase Series CG/CL/CQ Imperials are the most desirable Chryslers of the prewar years. The junior Eights and CH Imperial, while not in the same class are nonetheless highly desirable, especially in open body form.

Summary and Prospects

These cars have been steadily gaining in value over the past several decades and are so few in number that we can certainly look upon them as blue chip investments. If you can buy a CG/CL/CQ Imperial for half or less its fully restored value, the chances are that you can spend what it takes to get them into show condition and still have a car worth substantially more than you've put into it, particularly if it has a LeBaron or full-custom body. More caution has to be applied to smaller Eights, but the money it takes to acquire one is considerably less.

Specifications

Engines (net hp)
Type: cast-iron inline Eight, nine main bearings
240ci (3 x 4.25in), 82hp: CD Series built 1930
261ci (3.13 x 4.25in), 90hp: CD series built 1931
274ci (3.25 x 4.13in), 90-98hp: 1933 Royal
282ci (3.25 x 4.25in), 95hp: 1931 Deluxe Eight, 1932 CD
299ci (3.25 x 4.50in), 100-108hp: 1932 CP, 1933 Imperial CQ
385ci (3.50 x 5.00in), 125hp: 1931-33 Imperial CG/CH/CL

Chassis and Drivetrain
Ladder chassis, conventional clutch, shaft drive, four-wheel hydraulic brakes, wire wheels on CG, wood-spoke wheels on other 1931 models, wire wheels standard on all models 1932-33. Four-speed manual transmission with floor shift.

Size and Weight
Wheelbase (in):
1933 Royal 120in; 1931 CD & Deluxe 124in; 1932 CP Eight 125in; 1933 CQ Imperial 126in; 1932 CH Imperial 135in; 1931-32 CG Imperial 145in; 1932-33 CL Imperial 146in
Curb Weight (lb):
1931 Eights 3,100-3,600lb; 1932 CP Eights 3,700-4,100lb; 1933 CQ Imperials 3,750-4,150lb; CG/CH/CL Imperials 4,500-5,300lb

Production

	1931	1932	1933
**Eight roadster	1,462	0	0
**Eight coupe	3,000	1,220	1,259
**Eight convertible coupe	700	396	539
**Eight 4dr sedan	9,000	3,198	7,993
**Eight phaeton	85	0	0
**Eight convertible sedan	0	251	257
**Eight sedan 7passenger	0	0	246
**Eight chassis	108	48	95
Deluxe Eight roadster	*511	0	0
Deluxe Eight coupes 2/4passenger	*1,506	0	0
Deluxe Eight coupe 5passenger	*500	0	0
Deluxe Eight convertible coupe	*700	0	0
Deluxe Eight 4dr sedan	*5,843	0	0
Deluxe Eight phaeton	*113	0	0
Deluxe Eight chassis	*126	0	0
Imperial Eight coupe 2/4passenger	0	239	364
Imperial Eight coupe 5passenger	0	0	267
Imperial Eight 4dr sedan	0	1,002	2,584
Imperial Eight convertible coupe	0	0	243
Imperial Eight convertible sedan	0	152	364
Imperial Eight chassis	0	9	16
Imperial Custom roadster	*100	0	9
Imperial Custom phaeton	*85	0	36
Imperial Custom coupe	*135	0	3
Imperial Custom convertible coupe	*10	28	0
Imperial Custom 4dr sedan	*909	0	0
Imperial Custom close-coupled sedan	*1,195	57	43
Imperial phaeton	0	14	0
Imperial Custom sedan 7/8passenger	*403	35	21
Imperial Custom limousine	*271	32	22
Imperial Custom convertible sedan	*25	49	11
Imperial Custom chassis	*95	5	6

*Model CG, extended into 1932 model year
** Base Eight. 1931-32 CD, 1932 CP, 1933 CT Royal

Return on investment (95-point condition 1):

	1980	1995	*Return
19331-32 CG LeBaron roadster	$130,000	$350,000	9.4%
1933 Royal convertible	$25,000	$35,000	2.5%

*compound annual rate of return unadjusted for maintenance, insurance, and running costs

Chapter 4

Airflow
1934-37

From the very beginning, engineering had been Chrysler's strong suit, so it was no surprise that the 1934 Chrysler Airflow was a product of engineers. What *was* curious was that canny businessmen like Walter Chrysler and K. T. Keller approved this advanced, art-deco creation without anything approaching a market study in one of the most dismal periods for the car industry, with the economy flat and even the new ideas of the Roosevelt Administration failing to turn things around. The Airflow was not only Walter Chrysler's first serious mistake, but a colossal marketing disaster for any firm, especially in the Depression.

A long-running story has it that Carl Breer got the idea for a streamlined car when he saw a squadron of Army Air corps planes flying overhead in 1927. In any event, Breer got together with Zeder and Skelton to consider an automobile employing aircraft design principles. Wind tunnel tests suggested its shape: a teardrop altered to allow for hood and windshield. A forward-mounted engine (directly over the front axle) allowed a capacious interior, and a strong beam-and-truss body provided

Early production or late prototype Series CU Chrysler Airflow sedan on its presentation stage. Carl Breer applied latest aircraft and automotive standards of construction and aerodynamics to the Airflow, which had been developing at Chrysler since 1927. Basic Airflow Eights all listed at $1,345; the majority were four-door sedans. *Publications International Ltd.*

A more conventional grille reminiscent of Ford products marked the 1935 Airflows, most of which were Imperials. The middle-priced C-2 range included two- and four-door sedans, the majority of which were four-doors like this. *Publications International Ltd.*

rigidity. The Airflow's seats were 50in wide, which was pretty impressive for the time; it had more head, hip, shoulder, and legroom than even big Walter Chrysler needed. Exterior styling, by Oliver Clark, followed the dictates of the engineers. While Chrysler did offer a conventional looking Six, all of its Eights in 1934 were Airflows. The Custom Imperial was the best looking because its long wheelbase allowed the rounded body to be stretched out more than the smaller models. From an aesthetic point of view the basic styling needed every inch it could get. To its credit, the Airflow delivered outstanding performance. In 1934 an Imperial coupe ran 95.7mph for the flying mile and 90mph for 500 miles at the Bonneville Salt Flats, capturing seventy-two national speed records in the process. Airflows weren't flimsy either: in Pennsylvania, one was purposely driven off a 110ft cliff, landed wheels down, and was driven away. The Airflow's main problem was its unorthodox shape—and an initial scarcity of cars in the dealerships, a dash of cold water following heavy Chrysler promotion. It was, in its way, the first "cab forward" Chrysler.

Because of the considerable retooling necessary to convert to Airflow production, Chrysler delayed the cars' appearance until January 1934; Custom Imperials didn't arrive until June. Lack of cars blunted public interest and created rumors that the Airflow had bugs. Weird looks did the rest, and in a year that saw most Detroit companies increase production by 40-60 percent, Chrysler's volume rose just 20 percent and continued to lag behind its chief competitors. Oldsmobile, which Chrysler had almost caught in the early 1930s, outproduced Chrysler two to one in 1934 and three to one in 1935.

Detroit lead times are long and it takes several years to alter a plan once it is in motion. Chrysler had banked heavily in the Airflow to inspire the design and sales of its cheaper makes. This having failed, a more conventional "Airstream" line of Sixes and Eights was hastened into production (see next chapter). Though not pure Airflow in design, their bodies had pontoon fenders, raked-back radiators, and teardrop headlamp pods. Then again, so did almost every '35 model. Given the amount they had invested in it, Chrysler reacted quickly and bit the bullet to scrub the Airflow and get back to a resolutely conventional style. The firm had been badly burned, and for twenty years would produce the most conservatively styled cars in the industry. Ironically, the Airflow only predicted the general shape of American cars six to eight years hence.

Identification

1934: Alligator hood with grille bars spilling onto its leading edge; recessed headlamps in teardrop shaped housing incorporating parking lights; triple bar bumpers; sloping V-type windshield; power brakes on Imperials.

1935: Squared off grille ends at radiator top instead of spilling over onto the hood; revised hood extends forward in a V-shape; single bar bumpers.

1936: Rounded barrel-style grille; humped trunk compartment; egg-crate type side hood vents; vertically adjustable seats.

1937: Hood is more conventional in style and extends prominently on top of a conventional barrel grille; horizontal hood louvers decorated with brightwork beading; headlamps mounted on the sides of the front hood; "Chrysler Airflow" script on panel above grille.

Appraisal

There were no open Airflows, so the avid acquisitive urge rag tops always provide is missing in this group of Chryslers. The smaller models have appreciated reasonably well over the last twenty years, and a really show-stopping example can now command $30,000, although you can pick up restorable ones for a tenth that. Imperials are considerably more valuable, although I disbelieve some price guide figures which state values like $150,000 for four-door sedans: even that long wheelbase isn't worth that kind of money, and I have seen no such Airflows advertised for sale. Of course, they made so few of these that it's unlikely I would. Ordinary Imperials cost as much as $50,000 for coupes in prime condition, but sedans are worth little more than half that.

Summary and Prospects

As we begin to understand the crucial importance of automotive aerodynamics, the Airflow takes on more historical interest. Whatever one thinks of its styling, it was a beautifully built and rugged beast, and the interiors are both sumptuous and neoclassic with their handsome art deco dashboards (the '37 has one of the industry's first "safety dashboards," with recessed instruments and extensive padding).

Return on investment (95-point condition 1):

	1980	1995	*Return
1934 Airflow sedan	$10,000	$30,000	7.6%
1934 Airflow Custom Imperial	$40,000	$120,000	7.6%

*compound annual rate of return unadjusted for maintenance, insurance and running costs

Production

	1934	1935	1936	1937
Eight coupe	732	379	110	230
Eight brougham	306	0	0	0
Eight 4dr sedan	7,226	4,617	1,590	4,370
Eight town sedan	125	0	0	0
Imperial coupe	212	200	240	0
Imperial 4dr sedan	1,997	2,398	4,259	0
Imperial town sedan	67	0	0	0
Imperial chassis	1	0	1	0
Imperial long wb 4dr sedan	25	69	38	0
Imperial long wb town sedan	1	1	0	0
Imperial long wb limousine	78	2	10	0
Imperial long wb sedan-limo	2	53	0	0
Custom Imperial sedan, 8passenger	17	15	0	0
Custom Imperial town sedan	28	0	0	0
Custom Imperial sedan-limo	20	15	37	0
Custom Imperial town-limo	2	2	0	0

Specifications
Engines (net hp)
Type: cast-iron inline Eight, nine main bearings
299ci (3.25 x 4.50in), 122hp: 1934 Eight
324ci (3.25 x 4.88in), 115hp: 1935-36 Eight
324ci (3.25 x 4.88in 130hp (138 optional 1935): 1934-36 Imperial,
1936 Custom Imperial, 1937 all Airflows
385ci (3.50 x 5.00in), 150hp: 1934-35 Custom Imperial

Chassis and Drivetrain
Ladder chassis, conventional clutch, shaft drive, four-wheel hydraulic brakes (vacuum assisted on Custom Imperial), steel disc wheels on touring, steel wheels. Three-speed manual transmission with floor shift, four-speed on Custom Imperial.

Size and Weight
Wheelbase (in.):
1934-36: Eight 123in; Imperial 128 and 137.5in; Custom Imperial 146in 1937: 128in
Curb Weight (lb):
Eights about 3,700lb; Imperials 4,150-4,500lb; Custom Imperials 5,700-6,000lb 1937 models 4,200-4,300lb

Chapter 5

Airstream & Royal
1935-39

Walter Chrysler turned the presidency over to K.T. Keller in 1935, and that conservative businessman immediately made himself felt. Though Chrysler wanted to continue the Airflow, Keller would have been happy to give it an immediate axe (he succeeded in 1937). In the meantime, he happily attached himself to those Airflow-substitutes already being planned and built when he became president of the corporation.

The new "Airstream" line of Chryslers and DeSotos was largely designed by the accomplished coachbuilder, Raymond H. Dietrich, who had joined Chrysler styling staff in 1934—and in those days the lead time for a new body was only a year. Dietrich's arrival at Chrysler is historically pivotal, because he almost singlehandedly elevated Chrysler's Art & Color Department to the same level of importance as Harley Earl's department of

What hath Ray wrought? Raymond H. Dietrich, brought in to help design-away the curse of the Airflow, helped create the 1935 Airstream series, which soon dominated Chrysler production. Two '35s demonstrate the more conventional look of the Airstream (left) versus the brilliant but unsalable Airflow. Yet the Airstream offered an all-steel unit body and styling that was certainly streamlined for its age. *Publications International Ltd.*

the same name at General Motors. The Airstream's speedy completion and quick production startup was a dramatic demonstration of Chrysler's ability to respond quickly to changing market conditions. Overall, there was a strong family resemblance to the Airflow, but it wasn't as far out and thus far more acceptable. It also offered a broader array of models and body styles.

Although the Airflow was substantially revised, the '35 and '36 Airstreams carried Chrysler Division: a Six on the 118in wheelbase, and an Eight on 121in, plus an extended wheelbase for the seven-passenger sedans. Power came from in-line engines offering up to 100hp in the Six and 110hp in the Eight. Chrysler total model year production was about 38,000 and 60,000 units respectively in the two years. In 1937 Chrysler announced a new line of bodies engineered by itself rather than Briggs, though Briggs continued to build them. Boasting one-piece roof construction, the '37 shells were retained with a minor facelift for 1938 and a major one for 1939. The Airstream Six became the Royal, which inherited the long wheelbase chassis, the Airstream Eight having been dropped in 1937 and the rest of the Chrysler line being devoted to Imperials and the last batch of Airflows. The Royal continued on stretched wheelbases for 1938 and 1939; in the latter year a more deluxe sub-model arrived called Windsor, a name that would remain part of the Chrysler line-up for nearly a quarter century.

These smooth running, good looking junior Chryslers were the Division's bread and butter cars through the late 1930s, good enough for around tenth place in the annual production race. After a slowdown during the 1938 recession, production at 92,000 was almost back to the 1937 pace when Chrysler set a record of 106,120 units.

The year of greatest progress was 1939, when a heavy facelift saw fender-mounted headlights, smooth luggage compartments melded into the fastback rear end, narrow running boards, and a prominent hood profile reminiscent of the "shark-nose" Grahams. An important '39 development was "Superfinish," the mirror-polishing of all chassis components which drastically reduced friction and wear. "Cruise-Climb" overdrive and column-mounted gearshift were options. Instrument panels were generally of the symmetrical type except in 1937, when the gauges were neatly grouped in front of the driver. The crack-open windshield disappeared in 1938, except on export models.

Identification

1935: All-steel unit body with convex, Ford-like grilles, horizontal hood lovers, sloping rear panels with built-in luggage compartments. Eights had a longer wheelbase and winged "8" emblem on hood sides; chrome trimmed running boards on Deluxe Eights.

1936: Oval diecast grille with vertical blades; teardrop-shaped hood louvers with horizontal bars and a prominent horizontal molding wrapped around the top of the nose; torpedo shaped parking lights matched the shape of the headlamps.

1937: New, rounded styling with less skirted and more curved fenders; horizontal bar hood side louvers wrapped around the nose; multiple horizontal bar grille. New instrument panel with gauges grouped in front of the driver.

1938: Grille was shield-shaped, tapering at the bottom, with thick vertical center molding and "Chrysler Royal" script on hood; headlamps mounted on fenders for first time instead of flanking the radiator; central mounted parking brake; deluxe steering wheel with horn ring. Twin glove compartments in symmetrical style dashboard.

1939: Headlamps built flush into fenders; V-shaped windshield; prow-shaped hood with horizontal bars combined with waterfall lower grille of vertical bars; "Chrysler" script on hood sides ("Chrysler Windsor" script on Windsor models).

Appraisal

The most desirable juniors of this period are the Airstream Eights of 1935-36, which rode expansive wheelbases, were more luxuriously trimmed than the Sixes, and are more capable road cars and more fun to drive. Curiously, prices for open Airstreams do not vary much between Six and Eight, probably because all of them are so rare: $30,000 is about tops for a convertible or convertible sedan, while half that will buy a very good older restoration. Open Royals were built only in 1937-38, and sell for about $25,000 tops in the present market. Closed models run around $12,000 to $15,000 for the best showworthy examples and much less for closed bodies. The best buy of the lot would be an Airstream Eight rumble seat coupe at only $15,000—not a "Classic" in Classic Car Club parlance, but certainly a rakish late-thirties example of the art deco school. For connoisseurs of styling, the '39s have it all over the earlier cars, yet

A rounded vertical bar grille and more streamlined body styling marked the Airstream for 1936. The six-cylinder line included nearly 500 of these handsome convertible coupes, prime examples of the art deco school; not more than a handful exist today. *Publications International Ltd.*

none of them cost more than $15,000 today, and a good one can be had for half that. Custom bodies were rare on junior Chryslers, but Derham executed a handsome town car in 1938 which would be a real prize if you can find one. A '39 worth searching out is the handsome semi-custom coupe by Hayes of Grand Rapids, Michigan, a pretty Chrysler distinguished by its thin side window frames and 2+2 seating, with twin auxiliary folding rear seats.

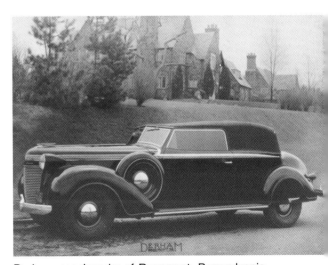

Derham coachworks of Rosemont, Pennsylvania, created this handsome convertible Victoria on one of only 118 Imperial Eight chassis released for special bodies in 1937. The rounded deck and Victoria top with formal quarters were typically Derham. Like all late custom-bodied Chryslers, this would be highly desirable today. *Publications International Ltd.*

For 1938 a cleaner bisected horizontal bar grille was applied and Imperials carried little chevrons on the front fenders. The vast majority were sedans like this 144in-chassis Custom Imperial. *Publications International Ltd.*

Summary and Prospects

There are not a lot of these Chryslers around; I can count the number of open Airstreams I've tracked over the past several years on one hand, and because of this asking prices vary wildly, some being far higher than the price guides say you should consider paying. This leads to the conclusion that, "bought right," an Airstream or Royal in an open body style or at least a coupe would be an excellent investment. Expect to have a lot of trouble finding body parts and hardware, however.

Its own unique grille marked the New York Special for 1938, progenitor of the long-lived Chrysler New Yorker. Though built on the C19 Imperial chassis it was considered a Chrysler; yet it carried Imperial trim and cost several hundred dollars more than comparable Chryslers ($1,450 as shown, with side-mount spares). A business coupe was planned in this series, but not built. In 1939 it blossomed into the New Yorker line, which would become a Chrysler standard. *Publications International Ltd.*

Return on investment (95-point condition 1):

	1981	1995	*Return
1935 Airstream Eight convertible	$10,000	$30,000	8.0%
1937 Royal convertible sedan	$20,000	$30,000	2.8%
1939 Royal Windsor coupe by Hayes	$5,300	$14,000	7.0%

*compound annual rate of return unadjusted for maintenance, insurance, and running costs

Specifications

Engines (net hp)
Type: cast-iron inline Six with four main bearings and Eight with five main bearings.
6-cylinder, 241.5ci (3.38 x 4.50in), 93-100hp (1935-36 Six)
6-cylinder, 228.0ci (3.38 x 4.25in), 93-100hp (1937), 95-102hp
(1938-39)
8-cylinder, 273.8ci (3.25 x 4.13in), 105-110hp (1935-36 Eight)

Chassis and Drivetrain
Ladder chassis, conventional clutch, shaft drive, four-wheel hydraulic brakes, steel spoke wheels. Three-speed manual transmission with floor shift, column shift and overdrive optional 1939.

Size and Weight
Wheelbase (in):
Airstream Six, 1935-36: 118in; Airstream Eight, 1935-36: 121in, long chassis 133in; Royal, 1937: 116in, long chassis 133in; Royal, 1938-39: 119in, long chassis 136in
Curb Weight (lb):
Airstream Six 2,900-3,100lb; Airstream Eight 3,100-3,500lb; Royal 3,050-3,600lb

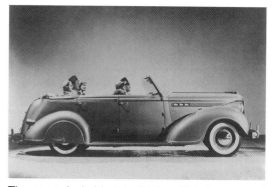

The most desirable late thirties Chryslers are, of course, individual customs in open body styles, like this phaeton on the Custom Imperial chassis. Only eleven of those long-wheelbase chassis were produced for custom bodies; the rest carried sedan or limo factory bodies. *Publications International Ltd.*

A most desirable late prewar Chrysler is the semi-custom Imperial Eight coupe by Hayes Body Corporation of Grand Rapids, Michigan. Only thirty-five Hayes Imperials were built, although the coachworks produced other coupes on the junior chassis. *Publications International Ltd.*

Production

	1935	1936	1937	1938	1939
Six (1935-36), Royal (1937-39)					
business coupe, 2pass.	1,975	3,703	9,830	4,830	*4,780
coupe, 2/4pass.	861	759	1,050	363	*239
Windsor club coupe, 5pass.	0	0	0	0	2,983
touring brougham	1,901	3,177	7,835	3,802	4,838
fastback brougham	0	0	750	88	0
fastback 4dr sedan	6,055	0	1,200	112	0
touring 4dr sedan	12,790	34,099	64,408	31,991	*45,955
fastback 2dr sedan	400	0	0	0	0
convertible coupe	0	650	767	480	0
convertible sedan	0	497	642	177	0
long wb sedan, 7pass.	0	0	856	722	621
long wb sedan-limo, 7pass.	0	0	138	161	191
chassis	476	586	524	564	394
Eight (all called "Deluxe" in 1936)					
business coupe	100*	520	0	0	0
coupe, 2/4passenger	550*	325	0	0	0
touring brougham	500*	268	0	0	0
4dr sedan	2,958	0	0	0	0
touring sedan	4,394	6,547	0	0	0
Deluxe conv. coupe	101	240	0	0	0
Deluxe conv. sedan	0	362	0	0	0
Deluxe Traveler long wb sedan	245	350	0	0	0
Deluxe long wb sedan, 7passenger	212	619	0	0	0
Deluxe long wb sedan-limo	0	67	0	0	0
Deluxe long wb Town sedan	0	8	0	0	0
chassis	237	196	0	0	0

* combined standard and Deluxe (1935), standard and Windsor (1939);
Chrysler records do not break out these sub-models. The 1939 figure includes a handful of Hayes coupes, probably not more than twenty.

★★★

Chapter 6

Imperial, New Yorker, & Saratoga 1937-39

Two more famous Chrysler model names were established in the late thirties: the New Yorker, stemming from the Imperial sub-model "New York Special" of 1938; and the Saratoga, another sub-model spun off the '39 Imperial. Though mounted on the Imperial's chassis, the New York Special carried its own prominent barrel grille, with a handsome interior of color keyed paint, upholstery, and carpeting throughout. Dealers and buyers alike immediately referred to this model as the "New Yorker," and so it became for 1939, still within the Imperial range but offered in four different body styles. Contrary to later practice, both the '38 and '39 New Yorkers were priced about $100 higher than the standard Imperials, owing to their special trim and upholstery. The '39s, which had two-tone "drawing room" upholstery color keyed to internal paintwork, included about thirty-five examples of the Imperial Hayes-built coupe, a very good looking semi-custom with thin side window frames and small auxiliary seats mounted behind the front seats. (The Hayes coupe was also catalogued in the Royal Windsor line.)

The 1939 Saratoga, offered as a coupe or sedan, cost still more money: at just short of $1,500 it was the most expensive Chrysler in the line. Its distinction was chiefly its upholstery, a luxurious combination of leather and Bedford cord. The Saratoga quickly gained a reputation as a car for the sporting driver (or at least the driving sport), and it was fitting that the same badge went on the fastest versions of Chrysler's hemi-head V-8 when that powerful brute was announced in 1951.

When the Airflow flopped earlier, Chrysler launched the lower priced Airstreams to regain lost ground, but the Imperial labored on for two years strictly as an Airflow. The first conventional Imperials arrived for 1937 on the old Airstream Eight chassis, handsomely facelifted by the talented Ray Dietrich and lavishly equipped to out-appeal their upper middle priced competition, chiefly Buick. A top-line range of Custom Imperials on a new 140in wheelbase was also fielded, and taken up to an incredible 144in in 1938-39. Custom Imperials supposedly had to be individually ordered, though the quantity of seven-passenger sedans belies this. They were confined to closed cars, and a handful of chassis were provided to custom body builders.

A gem from the late prewar period, this Imperial town car by LeBaron is in the custom-bodied and chauffeur-driven tradition. *Publications International Ltd.*

Another 1939 Imperial with a European flair, this cabriolet by de Corvaia was auctioned a few years ago in Paris at the height of the investment boom, an extremely desirable one-off. *Jan Norbye*

Identification

1937: Same styling as Royal with longer hood and cowl: barrel grille composed of horizontal bars and horizontal hood louvers; crank type windshield, safety instrument panel with gauges grouped in front of driver, and no protruding knobs.

1938: Shield-shaped grille, tapering at the bottom, with thick vertical center molding; chrome chevrons on front fender moldings headlamps mounted on fenders for first time instead of flanking the radiator; central mounted parking brake; deluxe steering wheel with horn ring. Twin glove compartments in symmetrical style, polished woodgrain dashboard. New York Special: unique grille with every other bar painted black, special upholstery, and Custom Imperial engine.

1939: Headlamps built flush into fenders; V-shaped windshield; prow-shaped hood with horizontal bars combined with waterfall lower grille of vertical bars (wider than this grille on Royals). New Yorker: two-tone cloth upholstery. Saratoga: Bedford cord and leather upholstery. Custom Imperial: dashboard keyed to upholstery color. Badges were color keyed to model.

Appraisal

Little seen and not appreciated as widely as they ought to be, senior Chryslers from the late thirties offer today's collectors fine craftsmanship and engineering along with luxury for relatively little money. Quality of fit and finish is of a high order, and there are many desirable sub-models, notably the Hayes coupe, the New York Special, the 1939 New Yorker series, and of course the Saratoga. Some very fine customs including a convertible Victoria and a fastback town car were built, mostly by Derham, on Custom Imperial chassis.

From the collector standpoint it's a shame that so few Imperials (and no New Yorkers or Saratogas) were offered in open body styles: a mere 1,500 convertible coupes and convertible sedans in two model years only. This has kept this class of Chrysler from really zooming in value on the old car market; conversely it has left a lot of very worthy cars around that are still relatively affordable.

Summary and Prospects

A number of Imperials wore custom bodies by Fleetwood, Locke, and others; these are commensurably more valuable than factory bodies, especially in open form. Still, overall, a collector car, not an investment.

Return on investment (95-point condition 1):

	1980	1995	*Return
1937 Imperial convertible sedan	$19,000	$30,000	3.1%
1937 Imperial Derham customs	$60,000	$95,000	3.1%
1938 New York Special 4dr sedan	$5,500	$15,000	7.0%
1938 Derham semi-customs, open	$27,500	$70,000	6.5%
1939 New Yorker coupe by Hayes	$5,800	$15,000	6.6%
1939 Saratoga club coupe	$4,900	$15,000	7.8%

*compound annual rate of return unadjusted for maintenance, insurance, and running costs

Production

	1937	1938	1939
Imperial:			
business coupe, 2pass.	1,075	*766	492
coupe, 2/4pass.	225	80	**35
convertible coupe	351	189	0
touring brougham	430	245	185
touring sedan	11,796	*8,554	*10,536
convertible sedan	325	113	0
New Yorker Victoria coupe	0	0	99
New Yorker business/ club coupe	0	0	606
Saratoga club coupe	0	0	134
chassis	118	55	48
Custom Imperial:			
4dr sedan, 5pass.	187	252	88
long wb sedan, 7pass.	721	122	95
sedan limo, 7pass.	276	145	117
chassis	16	11	7

*includes New York Special (1938), New Yorker, and Saratoga (1939)
** Hayes Victoria coupe (2+2)

Specifications

Engines (net hp)
Type: cast-iron inline Eight with five main bearings.
273.8ci (3.25 x 4.13in), 110-115hp (1937 Imperial)
298.7ci (3.25 x 4.50in), 110-122hp (1938 Imperial)
323.5ci (3.25 x 4.88in), 130-138hp (1938 Custom Imperial & New York Special, 1939 all models)

Chassis and Drivetrain
Ladder chassis, conventional clutch, shaft drive, four-wheel hydraulic brakes, steel spoke wheels. Three-speed manual transmission with floor shift, column shift and overdrive optional 1939.

Size and Weight
Wheelbase (in):
Imperial, 1937, 121in, 1938-39, 125in; Custom Imperial, 1937 140.0in; 1938-39 144.0in; New York Special, New Yorker and Saratoga, 125in
Curb Weight (lb):
Imperial 3,400-4,000lb; Custom Imperial 4,500-4,700lb; 1938 New York Special 3,500lb; 1939 New Yorker 3,600lb; 1939 Saratoga 3,650lb

★★

Chapter 7

Royal & Windsor
1940-49

The transition cars that brought Chrysler through the war years and on into the postwar era were designed (as were their predecessors) by Raymond H. Dietrich and Chrysler's Art and Color Department, counterpart to the similarly named GM group, but not nearly at the same leading edge of fashion. Chrysler styling was anything but radical: notchbacked, smooth at the front and rear, with prominent individual (bolt-on) fenders. Engineering continued to prevail over styling and was supported wholeheartedly by President K.T. Keller. The design that resulted, as one wag put it, wouldn't knock your eyes out but wouldn't knock your hat off either. The public agreed with Keller: in model year production during the 1940s, Chrysler never finished out of the top ten, and output of over 160,000 '41 models was a new Division record.

The bulk of Chryslers were junior models: the Royal and Windsor, mounted on wheelbases around 122in (plus a longer chassis for extended bodies) and powered by the faithful cast-iron Six, which entered 1940 at 95hp and 1949 at 114. The '40 models were good-looking, with a simple horizontal bar grille; style changes for '41 were minimal,

the grilles become simpler and the taillamps more ornate. Chrysler also issued a wide variety of upholstery in 1941. There was Highlander Plaid, which had debuted in 1940 on the New Yorker, a striking combination of Scots plaid and leatherette; Saran, a woven plastic and leatherette designed for certain open models; and Navajo, a pattern resembling the blankets of the Southwest Indians. One new mechanical feature was optional Vacamatic transmission, a self-shifter that operated between the two lower and two higher gears. Manual shifting was still required from low to high ranges.

A significant facelift marked the '42 models, where the grille's chrome bands were wrapped right around the front fenders. The hoodline looked sleeker than before and opened from the front instead of the side. The running boards were now hidden, concealed under flares at the bottom of the doors. Highlander Plaid was optional, and another special upholstery called Thunderbird again borrowed Indian motifs. Like other cars, Chryslers built after January 1st, 1942, used painted trim where chrome used to be, and in early February production shut down for the duration of World War II. During the war, Chrysler built anti-aircraft

A Windsor at the body-drop on the Jefferson Avenue production line just after World War II.

The bottom of the Chrysler line in 1946, the Royal business coupe came in at just under $1,500; inflation had brought its price up to nearly $1,900 by 1948. Coupes are prized for their scarcity and long-deck silhouette; scarcely 1,200 were built from 1946 through early 1949.

Royal internals: a four-door sedan shows that luxury was not entirely forgotten on the cheapest Chryslers, but a rubber mat was definitely *de rigueur* in the front.

guns, Wright Cyclone airplane engines, land mine detectors, radar units, marine engines, harbor tugs, and tanks—the latter its most famous product.

The postwar Royal and Windsor were, like all corporate products, facelifted versions of the '42s, except for front sheet metal, which featured new "fade-away" front fenders. Fender brightwork was reduced but grilles gained prominent vertical bars, a harmonica pattern that was one of the most highly chromed front ends in the industry. A Royal could be bought for little more than $1,000 in 1942, but with postwar inflation, the minimum price rose to nearly $1,500 in 1946, and would continue to rise through the end of the decade.

For 1947 there were only detail alterations to fender trim, hubcaps, colors, carburetion, wheels, and instruments. Goodyear low-pressure Super Cushion tires were adopted early in the model year, and the Windsor added the Traveler, a new luxury-utility car with special paint and interior and an attractive wooden luggage rack. Unlike the comparable DeSoto Suburban, the Traveler lacked fold-down seats and wooden rear floorboards and had a separate trunk compartment.

Chrysler's extravagant "jukebox" dashboard was one of the flashiest in the postwar period. Using solid and mottled plastics, it was a symmetrical affair with gauges at the left, a glovebox at right, and a huge radio speaker with a bank of control knobs in the middle. The knobs were clear Lucite; chrome plating was everywhere. The radio had a wonderful fat sound, thanks to a tone selector providing adjustment from "Mello" to "Speech," its dial changing from blue to red in the process. The 18in steering wheel had three spokes and an enormous chrome horn ring. At far left was

Not a Chrysler Traveler, but a Windsor with a roof rack, one of the long-wheelbase sedans from the early postwar period. Wheel "donuts" substituted for whitewalls until the tire industry recovered.

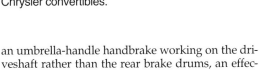

The most desirable model in this chapter, the Windsor convertible saw 5,000 copies in 1940-42 and 11,000 more in 1946-49. There are plenty to go round and they are among the most affordable Chrysler convertibles.

an umbrella-handle handbrake working on the driveshaft rather than the rear brake drums, an effective arrangement.

The 1948 line was a continuation of the '47, and Chrysler wasn't ready with its all-new 1949 models by autumn 1948; so from December to March the old models were offered again (the so-called "first series '49s,") though actual production of old-style models had ended before the New Year.

Identification

1940: More massive fenders than 1939, longer hood and wheelbase, flush fitting headlamps, nine horizontal grille bars, model name spelled out on each side of the hood.

1941: Similar to 1941, more glass front and rear, six horizontal grille bars more widely separated; Chrysler script nameplate on hood; available with and without runningboards.

1942: Grille bars extended around front fenders running back to wheel wells; one-piece alligator hood; concealed runningboards on all models; Highlander plaid interior was a $20 option on Windsor.

1946: New "harmonica" grille composed of vertical and horizontal bars; white taillamp buttons; high-beam indicator above speedometer. Fadeaway front fenders appear.

1947: As above but red taillamp buttons; also, the high-beam indicator moved to former position of left turn signal indicator (right indicator blinked for both left and right turns); larger rear wheelhouse openings.

1948: Identifiable only through serial numbers: 7002,674 to 70037180 on Royal; 70633017 to 70702442 on Windsor. Los Angeles Royals and Windsors ran from 67001001 to 67001920.

1949 "First Series": Identifiable only through serial numbers: 70031181 to 70038791 on Royal;

70702443 to 70717748 on Windsor. Los Angeles Royals and Windsors ran from 67001921 to 67003000.

Appraisal

The strongest collector interest among 1940-49 Royals and Windsors surrounds the convertible coupe, offered only as a Royal, and the only body style other than the Town & Country (which is covered in a separate chapter) worth over $20,000 in prime show condition today. Curiously, some price guides rate the 1942 convertible at only 80 percent the value of the '41 and postwar models, which is certainly odd: the '42 is both better looking and far scarcer. I was unable to track any asking prices but the '42 ragtop is certainly worth as much, and possibly more, than the other convertibles. Highlander plaid, Saran, Navajo, and Thunderbird upholstery was supposedly confined to two-door models but is occasionally found on four-door sedans as well. Highlander is the most common, and these models are distinguished by "Highlander" script in the nameplates on the sides of the hood. The other trim options are extremely rare and Navajo is the most sought after. Given today's computerized upholstery duplication capabilities, it can (and has, on one car I know) been "cloned." Such clones may be extremely difficult to identify as anything other than originals. Closed models tend to be very low priced; as little as $7,500 will buy a show winner. Coupes are preferable to sedans, and long-wheelbase cars enjoy a 50 percent premium over standard wheelbase examples.

Summary and Prospects

Never a high-flying collector car, the forties Royal/Windsor represents a beautifully built, quality product, not a substitute investment portfolio.

Chrysler enthusiasts like this just fine, and trade is brisk among devotees of the marque, especially among the far more numerous postwar models. Perhaps because of this, the postwar convertibles, which were a bargain fifteen years ago, have lately caught the prewar versions in value, which made them a superior investment in 1980. Right now, my money would be on the '42, which is bound to increase in value, if only you can find one. Among closed body styles, Royals are much scarcer in the postwar years, but because they are the bottom line model nobody much cares. Coupes are better proportioned than sedans and even long-wheelbase cars, and would be the best choice among closed body styles for today's collectors. Appreciation will continue at the present modest rate.

Return on investment (95-point condition 1):

	1980	1995	*Return
1940 Windsor convertible coupe	$10,000	$25,000	6.3%
1941 Windsor Highlander coupe	$5,000	$13,000	6.6%
1942 Windsor convertible coupe	$12,000	$28,000	4.8%
1946-49 Royal four-door sedan	$3,600	$8,500	5.9%
1946-49 Windsor convertible coupe	$6,000	$25,000	10.0%
1947-49 Windsor Traveler sedan	$3,800	$9,500	6.3%

*compound annual rate of return unadjusted for maintenance, insurance, and running costs

---

Specifications

Engines (net hp)
Type: cast-iron inline Six with four main bearings
241.5ci (3.38 x 4.50in), 108-115hp (1940-41)
250.0ci (3.44 x 4.50in), 120hp (1942), 114hp (1946-49)

Chassis and Drivetrain
Ladder chassis, conventional clutch, shaft drive, four-wheel hydraulic brakes, steel wheels. Three-speed manual transmission with floor shift, column shift, and overdrive optional 1940-42, Fluid Drive optional 1941-49.

Size and Weight
Wheelbase (in):
1940: 122.5 in; 1941-42: 121.5in; long wheelbase models 139.5in
Curb Weight (lb):
1940-42 Royal 3,000-3,300lb; 1940-42 Windsor 3,100-3,500lb; 1940-42 long wheelbase models 3,550-3,700lb; 1946-49 Royal 3,400-3,700lb; 1946-49 Windsor 3,500-3,800lb; 1946-49 long wheelbase models 3,900-4,100lb; 1947-49 Traveler 3,600lb

---

Production

	1940	1941	1942	1946-9
Royal 4dr sedan	23,274	51,378	7,424	24,279
Windsor 4dr sedan	28,477	36,396	10,054	161,139
Windsor convertible coupe	2,275	4,432	574	11,200
Royal club coupe	n/a	10,830	779	4,318
Windsor club coupe	n/a	8,513	1,713	26,482
Royal 2dr sedan (brougham)	n/a	8,006	709	1,117
Windsor 2dr sedan (brougham)	n/a	2,898	317	4,034
Royal business coupe	n/a	6,846	479	1,221
Windsor business coupe	n/a	1,921	250	1,980
Royal 4dr town sedan	n/a	1,277	73	0
Windsor 4dr town sedan	n/a	2,704	479	0
Royal/Windsor 2dr sedan	9,851	*	*	*
Royal/Windsor business coupe	5,117	*	*	*
Royal/Windsor coupe, 5pass.	4,315	*	*	*
Royal/Windsor long wb sedan	439	*	*	*
Royal/Windsor limo, 8pass.	98	*	*	*
Royal long wb sedan	n/a	297	79	626
Windsor long wb sedan	n/a	116	29	4,390
Royal limo, 8pass.	n/a	31	21	169
Windsor limo, 8pass.	n/a	54	12	1,496
Windsor Traveler (1947-49)	0	0	0	4,182
Royal/Windsor chassis	152	3	0	1

* separately broken out for 1942-49

Chapter 8

Saratoga, Traveler, and New Yorker 1940-49

Commencing with the 1940 model year, the previous broad line of Imperials was replaced by a much smaller range of long-wheelbase Crown Imperials, targeted mainly at the commercial market (see Chapter 10). The "senior" family-size Chryslers were now confined to the Saratoga, New Yorker, and, for 1940 only, the lower-priced Traveler. The 1940 chassis assigned to these models was numbered C-26, with a 128in wheelbase; from 1941 to the leftover "first series '49s," the wheelbase was half an inch shorter. Covered separately in Chapter 9 is the Town & Country, which sprang from the New Yorker line but soon acquired a persona all its own.

Like the junior Royal and Windsor, these were transition models designed by Raymond H. Dietrich and Chrysler's Art and Color Department. They lasted much longer than Chrysler had expected, since production shut down in February 1942 and there was no point in tooling anything different to get back in production when the war ended. Fadeaway front fenders and a new grille distinguished the postwar models.

Although these cars represent a small fraction of total Chrysler production, they are far more desirable, being longer, wider, more elegant looking, luxuriously turned out, and powered by eight-cylinder engines. All of them, in fact, carried the well-developed 323.5ci L-head with about 135-145hp. Styling changes were evolutionary, sticking to the horizontal bar theme in prewar years and adopting a bold egg-crate grille for the postwar period. A convertible model, which had been missing in 1939, returned to the New Yorker. Highlander Plaid, a striking and imaginative interior upholstery option, was introduced in 1940 on the New Yorker coupe and convertible; it was followed by Saran plastic and leatherette and the rare Navajo and Thunderbird Indian patterns.

Mounted on what was essentially a New Yorker chassis were two limited edition 1941 showcars. The Thunderbolt, designed by Alex Tremulis, was a predictive three-seater with an envelope body and a retractable hardtop covering its single bench seat. It featured hidden headlamps, electric window lifts and deck opener, pushbutton doors, and Bedford cord upholstery. Designed to wow the showgoing public, the Thunderbolt would later inspire postwar styling. Built alongside it was the Newport parade phaeton, with dual cockpits and windshields, also equipped with hidden headlamps and handleless doors. Four Newports are known to exist; there is at least one Thunderbolt. Either one is, of course, highly desirable: the most costly and sought after Chryslers of the decade.

Introduced on the 1939 Imperials, Fluid Drive quickly gained adherents and was found on most senior Chryslers of this period. A semi-clutchless transmission, it consisted of two turbine fans running opposite each other in an oil bath, mounted between clutch and flywheel. The shift lever could be moved in one "drive" position and the car stopped and started without the use of the clutch pedal.

Most year-to-year changes were made up front: the tall 1940 grille was lowered and widened for 1941, then wrapped around the front end for 1942. The '41 running boards were hidden, concealed under flares at the bottom of the doors.

Ornate and magnificent, the Saratoga dashboard of the postwar years. This car is without the radio; the panel with "Saratoga" script popped out to admit its controls. Note the imaginative use of mottled and clear plastic, a wonder material in those years.

Typical of the senior Forties Chrysler, the Saratoga four-door sedan sold for about $2,000 to $2,300 in the early postwar years; only 4,611 of these were produced, and less of the other Saratoga body styles.

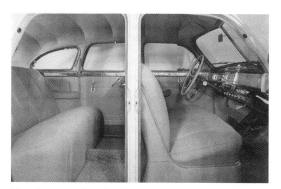

The Saratoga interior: finer materials than the Royal and Windsor, but still a rubber mat up front. You had to move up to a Traveler or New Yorker to get full carpeting.

A few over 4,000 Chrysler Travelers were built in the early postwar period. The roof rack was a strongly built affair of plated metal and wood. Chrysler name on hubcaps signifies a 1947 or later model.

The Traveler's interior was built for abuse, upholstery being a combination of Saran plastic and leather; carpets ran full width and color was used imaginatively; note also that beautiful marbled dashboard.

Some models built after January 1st, 1942, used painted instead of chrome trim. One of the gaudiest grilles in the industry arrive on the 1946 model and was continued unchanged through the "first series" '49s, which were leftover '48s sold as stopgaps until the redesigned "second series" arrived in late March 1949.

Only a handful of postwar senior Chryslers were Saratogas and the New Yorker dominated production. There were only five body styles: two sedans, two coupes, and the New Yorker convertible. The town sedan was not produced by Chrysler Division after the war.

Identification

1940: More massive fenders than 1939, longer hood and wheelbase, flush fitting headlamps, nine horizontal grille bars, model name spelled out on each side of the hood.

1941: Similar to 1941, more glass front and rear, six horizontal grille bars more widely separated; Chrysler script nameplate on hood; available with and without running boards.

1942: Grille bars extended around front fenders running back to wheel wells; one-piece alligator hood; concealed running boards on all models.

1946: New "harmonica" grille composed of vertical and horizontal bars; white taillamp buttons; high-beam indicator above speedometer.

1947: As above but red taillamp buttons and high-beam indicator moved to former position of left turn signal indicator (right indicator blinked for both left and right turns); larger rear wheelhouse openings.

1948: Identifiable only through serial numbers: 6768486 to 6770180 on Saratoga; 7405174 to 7408109 on New Yorker/Town & Country.

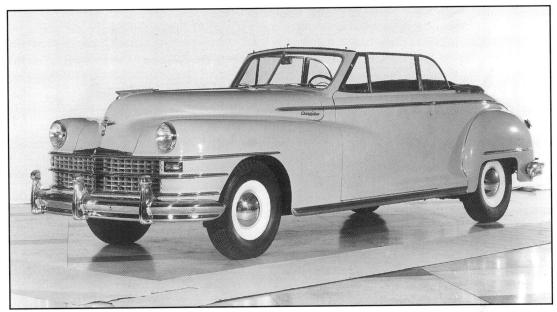

Top of the line New Yorker in its most desirable body style, of which only 3,000 were built. The longer wheelbase does much to enhance these luxurious Chryslers.

1949 "First Series": Identifiable only through serial numbers: 6770181 to 6770612 on Saratoga; 7408110 to 7408483 on New Yorker/Town & Country.

Appraisal

The New Yorker convertible, especially with one of the optional upholstery combinations, is clearly the most collectible senior Chrysler from the 1940-49 period (other than the Town & Country). Derham built a handful of highly customized convertibles in 1941-42 with Darrin-like cut-down doors, and these are 50 percent more valuable than standard convertibles. Like Windsors from the same period, some price guides rate the '42 New Yorker convertibles as much as $6,000 below 1941, which makes no sense at all. Highlander plaid, Saran, Navajo, and Thunderbird upholstery was supposedly confined to two-door models but is occasionally found on four-door sedans as well. Highlander is the most common, and these models are distinguished by "Highlander" script in the nameplates on the sides of the hood. The other trim options are extremely rare and Navajo is the most sought after. (See notes about cloning these upholstery patterns in this section of the preceding chapter.) Closed models are much less costly than convertibles but the coupes lead the sedans by $3,000 or $4,000, all other conditions being equal. There are no special long-wheelbase models among the 1940-49 Saratoga and New Yorker, these being confined

Last of the prewar New Yorkers, the '42 is rare indeed today. This is a four-door sedan, the most popular model, which sold 7,042 copies.

to the Crown Imperial line.

Summary and Prospects

Prewar New Yorker convertibles were once worth more than postwar, but today they all command close to $30,000 in absolutely pristine show condition; yet a decent one can be bought for less than half that and it's relatively inexpensive to restore thanks to bolt-on fenders and a fairly adequate supply of parts. All models are very good buys on the current market, not extravagantly priced except possibly for the Derham custom convertibles. They are gaudily turned out but built with abundant quality of

Interior of a New Yorker finished in Chrysler's inimitable Highlander Plaid combined with Saran plastic. There was nothing quite like it, and this photo should explain why collectors look for this special interior on forties models.

Specifications
Engines (net hp)
Type: cast-iron inline Eight with five main bearings.
8cyl, 323.5ci (3.25 x 4.88in), 135hp, 143hp optional (1940)
8cyl, 323.5ci (3.25 x 4.88in), 137hp, 140hp optional (1941)
8cyl, 323.5ci (3.25 x 4.88in), 140hp (1942)
8cyl, 323.5ci (3.25 x 4.88in), 135hp (1946-49)

Chassis and Drivetrain
Ladder chassis, conventional clutch, shaft drive, four-wheel hydraulic brakes, steel wheels. Three-speed manual transmission with column shift, 1940; Fluid Drive optional 1940 and 1946, standard in other model years.

Size and Weight
Wheelbase (in): 128.5in (Thunderbolt 127.5in), 1940; 127.5in, 1941-49.
Curb Weight (lb): 3,600-4,100lb

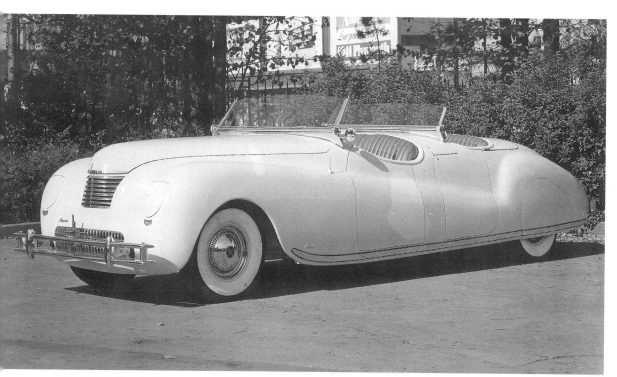

Also in 1940, six Newport parade phaetons were produced, with dual cockpits and windshields. Coachwork was by LeBaron. Four of these are known to have survived. They exercised a design influence similar to Virgil Exner's Imperial parade phaetons of the mid-fifties.

fine materials, and they function well. Look especially hard for Highlanders, they command a 20-30 percent premium over comparable standard-upholstery models and they always command a crowd of admirers at car shows. They are not going to zoom in value, but they provide a lot of car for the money. Also, for those who like rarity, check some of the production figures. One hundred fifty-five of something isn't a lot, yet that's the sum total of Saratoga broughams for 1946 through the first half of 1949.

Return on investment (95-point condition 1):

	1980	1995	*Return
1941 Thunderbolt/ Newport	$30,000	$350,000	17.9%
1940-42 New Yorker convertible	$12,000	$28,000	5.8%
as above, Highlander trim	$14,000	$35,000	6.3%
1946-49 New Yorker convertible	$9,500	$28,000	7.5%
1941-42 Derham custom convertible	$18,000	$40,000	5.5%
New Yorker club coupe	$4,500	$14,000	7.9%
Saratoga four-door sedan	$3,500	$9,500	6.9%
1940 Traveler coupe, 3passenger	$4,800	$11,000	5.7%

*compound annual rate of return unadjusted for maintenance, insurance, and running costs

Production

	1940	1941
sedan 4dr	14,603	15,868
town sedan 4dr (NY, Sar)	0	2,326
coupe	1,117	2,845
business coupe	731	771
sedan 2d (brougham)	275	293
convertible (NY)	845	1,295
Thunderbolt	0	6
Newport	0	6
chassis	0	9

Alex Tremulis's Chrysler Thunderbolt followed the "bar of soap" school of the time but was also predictive, with a retractable hardtop, hidden headlamps and electric servos for window lifts and decklid. It also clearly inspired 1942-48 Chrysler styling. Although six cars were built, one is known to the writer; has any reader seen another?

	1942	1946-49
Saratoga:		
business coupe	80	74
club coupe	193	765
sedan 2dr (brougham)	36	155
sedan 4dr	1,239	4,611
town sedan 4dr.	46	0
chassis	2	0
New Yorker:		
business coupe	158	701
club coupe	1,234	10,735
convertible	401	3,000
sedan 2dr (brougham)	62	545
sedan 4dr	7,045	52,036
town sedan 4dr	1,648	0
chassis	0	2

Chapter 9

Town & Country
1941-50

Although initially appearing as strictly a station wagon, the Town & Country was distinctive from the start. Instead of the typical 1940s woody, it was a smooth, fastback with double clamshell rear doors hinged at the sides—very streamlined indeed for 1941. It was conceivxed by the Boyertown, Pennsylvania, bodyworks, which had sent sketches to Chrysler Division president David Wallace. An improvement on the traditional wagon was Wallace's goal, and we may thus credit him with the first significant move toward the luxurious wagons of the postwar years.

Town & Countrys were built by Chrysler because its regular supplier, Briggs, lacked woodworking experience. The white ash framing was supplied by Pekin Wood Products of Arkansas, while the inner panels were initially Honduras mahogany; in late 1947 this was replaced by "Di-Noc," a mahogany-like decal. The 1941-42 T&C wagons rode on the shorter Windsor chassis, and was one

of the few models to sell better as a '42 than a '41. Because of a late start, Chrysler built only a handful of '41s but close to 1,000 '42 models.

After the war Chrysler removed its new nameplate from wagons and applied it to the most memorable Town & Countrys, the convertibles and sedans of 1946-48. Beloved by such celebrities as Clark Gable, Bob Hope, and Ray Milland, the T&C convertible became a kind of symbol of achievement in Hollywood, a glittering land yacht, often portrayed in the movies, one writer said, as the car driven by "the gambler or the other man, being considered perhaps too risqué for normal, upstanding heroes."

Chrysler had planned a fleet of 1946 Town & Countrys including a brougham (two-door sedan), roadster, and hardtop as well as the sedan and convertible. The first three were never released, though one brougham (its fate unknown) and seven hardtops (at least one still exists) were built experimentally. The Division settled on a four-door sedan and a convertible coupe, probably the most salable two body styles. The cars were beautifully turned out, with interlocking mitered corners, varnished to

The original 1941 Town & Country wagon sold for only $1,500 prewar dollars; fastback shape was a new development for the traditional depot hack body, and this pose emphasizes the future of transportation.

The '41 exposed, in nine-passenger configuration (most were sold this way), achieved with a folding bench seat; acres of varnished hardwood has to be maintained inside the car as well as out.

Unique semi-fastback metal roof and clamshell rear doors of the prewar Town & Country set it apart from the conventional. Although doors were simple and practical, lack of traditional tailgate hampered the loading of oversize cargo; most of these wagons were used by hotel and livery services rather than builders or tree surgeons.

The 1942 Town & Country wearing the sleek '42 facelift. Only about 1,000 of these were built, 85 percent in nine-passenger form. Roof rack does not appear to have been standard equipment, as the following photos indicate.

perfection: from the cowl back they were wood-bodied with the exception of the rear fenders and roofs. Equipment included two-speed electric wipers (a luxury in 1946), cut-pile carpeting, and, initially, spotlights. The sedan rear was very elaborate, different from all the other sedans; more customized even than the T&C convertible.

Chrysler built 8,368 T&C convertibles through the "first series" '49s and about half as many sedans, 100 of which were eight-cylinder models (1946 only).

The postwar Town & Country was distinguished for its interior, which was offered in a wide variety of upholstery including leather, Saran plastic, and Bedford cord, set off by rich grained wood paneling and color-keyed headliners, seat bolsters, and carpets. Wood decorated door panels and headliners of sedans, some of which came with a wooden luggage rack and roof runners (but these were changed to chrome-plated metal in June 1947 and became standard equipment in July.)

Few changes attended the 1947 and 1948/49 models, although they could be somewhat customized because so much of each car was built by hand. Though the sedan was still around, the convertible received most of the publicity. "Chrysler's work or play convertible," read one ad, was "magnificent in its utterly new styling, in the smooth, responsive power of Chrysler Gyro Fluid Drive and improved hydraulically operated transmission." From $2,800 in 1946, the convertible now cost $3,400, a stratospheric price for something other than an open Cadillac.

When Chrysler restyled for 1949, the Town & Country convertible remained in the line, still very beautiful but perhaps lacking some of the glitzy

character of its predecessors. A convertible and hardtop were planned for 1950, but only the hardtop appeared, priced at $4,003, the highest T&C yet. By then, however, Chrysler had reapplied the Town & Country name to station wagons, which were rapidly gaining in popularity, so the series of swank passenger cars ended after 1950. But the early T&C has retained its panache. There still aren't enough to go around, which is probably why the value keeps rising steadily.

Identification

Unmistakable with white ash and mahogany (or mahogany decal) paneling on sides and deck

Building the postwar Town & Country convertible. White ash framework was painstakingly cut and mitred together and the joins sanded to perfection; mahogany inserts later gave way to Di-Noc decal.

Three different approaches to the convertible's interior. The Town & Country was virtually a semi-custom, and a wide variety of Saran, leather, and cloth could be specified. Replicating it today is a challenge.

and Town & Country nameplates for all models.

1941: Station wagon only with clamshell doors, nine-bar grille.

1942: As above, with new five-bar '42 grille.

1946: Four-door sedan and convertible coupe bearing T&C badges. New "harmonica" grille composed of vertical and horizontal bars; white taillamp buttons; high-beam indicator above speedometer.

1947: As above but red taillamp buttons and high-beam indicator moved to former position of left turn signal indicator (right indicator blinked for both left and right turns); larger rear wheelhouse openings.

1948: Identifiable only through serial numbers: 7405174 to 7408109.

1949 "First Series": Identifiable only through serial numbers: 7408110 to 7408483. "Second Series"

all new boxy styling with busy grille encompassing Chrysler badge in molding on lower front edge of hood; special, flat taillamps, used since standard '49 taillamps would not have grafted to wood bodywork; convertible model only.

1950: Hardtop coupe model only; plainer grille with fewer horizontal and vertical bars; Chrysler badge now mounted on front of hood. Special flat taillights continued from 1949.

Appraisal

The beautiful wood trim adds grace and beauty to the familiar Chrysler lines, and the white ash framing adds structural rigidity. But upkeep is a problem. Shop manuals give detailed instructions, suggesting that a T&C be stripped and revarnished

The Town & Country sedan was offered on both the Windsor and New Yorker chassis with six- and eight-cylinder power respectively in 1946. From 1947 through early 1949 it was available only as an eight. Eyeballing the wheelbase on this one suggests it is an eight.

annually, with special attention to seams and corners where water enters the grain—these are clearly visible on many examples.

Summary and Prospects

Town & Countrys had stupendous gains in value during the boom years of the 1980s, especially convertibles, which were bid up to six-figure prices at some highly-touted auctions. They've settled down recently, but they all remain prime investments among special-interest cars. The greatest interest surrounds the 1946 to first series 1949 convertibles. Prewar wagons and 1949-50 T&Cs are worth commensurately less, but all are very good buys and strongly recommended.

The sedan interior was elaborately trimmed in leathers, plastics and hardwoods; note wooden headliner ribs and door panels and dark dashboard.

Specifications
Engines (net hp)
Type: cast-iron inline Six with four main bearings and Eight with five main bearings.
6-cylinder, 241.5ci (3.38 x 4.50in), 108-115hp (1941)
6-cylinder, 250.6ci (3.44 x 4.50in), 120hp (1942), 114hp (1946-49)
8-cylinder, 323.5ci (3.25 x 4.88in), 137-140hp (1941), 140hp (1942)
8-cylinder, 323.5ci (3.25 x 4.88in), 135hp (1946-50)

Chassis and Drivetrain
Ladder chassis, conventional clutch, shaft drive, four-wheel hydraulic brakes, steel wheels. Three-speed manual transmission with column shift, 1946; Fluid Drive optional, standard in other model years.

Size and Weight
Wheelbase (in):
121.5in (1941-48/9 6-cylinder); 127.5in (1941-48/9 8-cylinder); 131.5in (1949-50)
Curb Weight (lb):
3,600-3,700lb (1941-42); 3,900lb (1946-48/9 6-cylinder sedan); 4,300lb (1946-48/9 convertible); 4,000lb (1949-50).

Seven hardtop coupes were constructed using roof panels from the New Yorker club coupe; at least one survives today. As these factory photos indicate, the roofs were finished in padded vinyl or painted. These cars are hotly sought after and are likely to represent one instance when a closed body is more valued than an open body of the same model.

Another non-production T&C, the one-off 1946 brougham (two-door sedan) rode a 121.5in Windsor wheelbase and had six-cylinder power. This car's existence is unknown today; what a find it would be!

Return on investment (95-point condition 1):

	1980	1995	*Return
1941-42 station wagon	$17,000	$40,000	5.9%
1946-48 sedan, 6-cylinder	$11,000	$38,000	8.7%
1946 sedan, 8-cylinder	$14,000	$45,000	8.1%
1946-49 convertible	$25,000	$78,000	7.9%
1949 (2nd series) convertible	$21,000	$50,000	6.0%
1950 Newport hardtop	$12,000	$40,000	8.4%

*compound annual rate of return unadjusted for maintenance, insurance, and running costs

Although Chrysler contemplated a hardtop for 1949, the Town & Country returned again only as a convertible; the sedan version was dropped this year.

The ragtop sold for $4,000, more than most Cadillacs and about $600 more than the 1946-48 convertible.

For its final year except as a station wagon, the Town & Country was a Newport hardtop, priced the same as the previous year's convertible. Most were finished with a two-tone roof. Although lacking some of the custom-built qualities of its forebears, the '50 is still a tremendously impressive, good looking Chrysler.

Production

	1941	1942	1946	1947	1948/9
wagon, 9 pass., 6-cylinder	797	849	0	0	0
wagon, 6 pass., 6-cylinder	300	150	0	0	0
sedan, 6-cylinder	0	0	4,124	2,651	1,175
sedan, 8-cylinder	0	0	100	0	0
convertible, 8-cylinder	0	0	1,935	3,136	3,309
convertible, 6-cylinder	0	0	1	0	0
brougham (prototype)	0	0	1	0	0
hardtop (prototype)	0	0	7	0	0

	1949 (second series)	1950
convertible	1,000	0
Newport hardtop	0	700

Chapter 10

Crown Imperial
1940-49

Imperials of this period were long-wheelbase, mainly "professional" cars such as limousines and eight-passenger sedans. Although a number of interesting customs were built on the Crown chassis, and Imperial did list a six-passenger sedan, albeit on the same long wheelbase as the other bodies. A single 1940 chassis was supplied to Derham, who created a handsome parade phaeton; it can be seen today at the Henry Ford Museum in Dearborn, Michigan. Styling followed that of the junior models and the engine was Chrysler's familiar 323 straight Eight.

One exception to the long wheelbase was the special Town Sedan of 1941, which was mounted on a New Yorker chassis and priced at only $1,760, well down from the $2,500 or so it took to buy a larger Crown Imperial. Chrysler sold nearly 1,000

Town Sedans. The wonder was that they didn't keep the model in production for 1942, though production ended abruptly after Pearl Harbor.

After the war, Chrysler built 1,400 Crown Imperial limousines and eight-passenger sedans (limos without division windows) between 1946 and the first half of 1949. All of these shared the broad "dollar grin" grillework of the smaller Chryslers, the glittery dashboard festooned with chrome and the new miracle material called plastic, the rounded deck with prominent taillights sprouting from separate, bolt-on fenders. These were not cheap cars: they arrived in 1946 at close to $4,000 and by 1948 with postwar inflation they were priced well over $4,500. The same kind of money would buy a Cadillac Seventy-five or a Packard Custom Eight; the Crown Imperial didn't match Cadillac sales but outnumbered the long-wheelbase Packards by about five to one. Chrysler's (and Packard's) competitive failing was in chassis production, where they hardly registered, while Cadillac was producing upwards of 2,000 Series Seventy-five chassis for hearse, ambulance, and flower-car builders.

Identification

1940: More massive fenders than 1939, longer hood and wheelbase, flush fitting headlamps, nine horizontal grille bars, model name spelled out on each side of the hood.

1941: Similar to 1941, but long-wheelbase cars had curved, one-piece windshields (the first since 1934-36 Custom Imperials, which introduced them); more glass front and rear, six horizontal grille bars more widely separated; Chrysler script nameplate on hood; available with and without running boards.

1942: Grille bars not extended around front fenders as on other 1942 models; one-piece alligator hood; concealed running boards on all models.

1946: new "harmonica" grille composed of vertical and horizontal bars; white taillamp buttons; high-beam indicator above speedometer.

1947: As above but red taillamp buttons and high-beam indicator moved to former position of left turn signal indicator (right indicator blinked

The long-wheelbase (145.5in) Crown Imperial for 1946, here posed outside the Grosse Pointe, Michigan, yacht club, was the ultimate luxury carriage for Chrysler in the early postwar years. The build total for 1946-49 was only 750 sedans and 650 limousines, the latter fitted with a division window.

for both left and right turns); larger rear wheel-house openings.

1948: Identifiable only through serial numbers: 7810908 to 7811347.

1949 "First Series": Identifiable only through serial numbers: 7811348 and higher.

Appraisal

Jumbo long-wheelbase "professional" cars have a limited if enthusiastic following, and these Imperials are no exceptions. The most driveable and enjoyable is certainly the shorter Town Sedan of 1941, and this is also a relatively available model. Despite its high production figures, it has appreciated at a faster rate than the larger Imperials over the past fifteen years.

Summary and Prospects

Definitely for the collector and not the investor, this is not a place to put one's money with the thought of high returns, and restorations of such large luxury cars are bound to be expensive. On the other hand, many have been well treated throughout their lives, so it might not be necessary to contemplate serious restorations. Postwar models, which were worth less than prewar a couple of decades ago, have now matched the value of the latter, but are not likely to exceed it.

Return on investment (95-point condition 1):

	1980	1995	*Return
1940-42			
long-wheelbase	$6,000	$14,000	5.8%
1941 Town Sedan	$5,200	$14,500	7.1%
1946-49			
long-wheelbase	$4,300	$15,000	8.7%

*compound annual rate of return unadjusted for maintenance, insurance, and running costs

Production

	1940	1941	1942	1946/9
sedan, 4dr.	355	179	81	0
sedan, 4dr., 8pass.	2842	05	152	750
limousine	210	316	215	650
special town sedan				
(short wheelbase)	0	894	0	0
chassis	1	1	2	0

C39-S

Crown Imperial power was the same straight eight that drove the New Yorker and Saratoga, with 135hp. Virtually always equipped with Fluid Drive, the heavy Crowns were sluggish performers: but smoothness, not hot-rod acceleration, was what it delivered.

Specifications
Engines (net hp)
Type: cast-iron inline Eight with five main bearings.
323.5ci (3.25 x 4.88 in), 132-143hp (1940), 143hp (1941), 140hp (1942), 135hp (1946-49).

Chassis and Drivetrain
Ladder chassis, Fluid Drive standard.

Size and Weight
Wheelbase (in): 145.5in; 127.5in (1941 Town Sedan)
Curb Weight (lb): 4,300-4,900lb; 1941 Town Sedan 3,900lb

Chapter 11

Royal & Windsor
1950-54

My father played out the role Walter P. Chrysler had in mind for him when he assembled Chrysler Corporation in the 1920s, moving up step by step through the divisional hierarchy. Having nursed his '38 Plymouth two-door through the war, Dad sold it for more than he'd paid for it during the postwar car shortage. Then he started a new business and bought a new '49 Dodge Meadowbrook. The business having prospered by 1952, he moved up to a Chrysler Windsor, skipping DeSoto. (In 1955 he went back and bought a DeSoto because Chrysler prices appalled him, which was not, I think, the way W.P. and K.T. Keller had

planned. Worse, in 1958 he joined the stampede to Rambler, which I'm fairly certain was not something that would have pleased anybody at Chrysler.)

My dad always thought Chrysler built the best cars among the Big Three, and who was I to argue. The Windsor was as solid as Mount Everest, as roomy as a small hotel, smooth, and comfortable, though no powerhouse with Fluid Drive and the old Chrysler Six. This engine breathed its last in 1954, and Chrysler entered a V-8s only mode which would last for some time. For a few years in the sixties they would advertise that they'd never, but never, "build a small Chrysler," but nobody took them serious, even then.

For 1949-50, they were all ordinary six-cylinder family chariots, Royals and Windsors, boxy and upright, all sound as a drum. The convertibles were beautifully built, handsomely upholstered, and almost as solid as the closed bodies. The Royal was dropped in 1951 and a dual line of Windsor and Windsor Deluxe installed in its place; these continued until 1954, when Chrysler began to emphasize V-8s and the six-cylinder line shrank to just six Windsor Deluxe models. Prices for the everyday four-door sedans ran around $2,500 for Windsors, a few hundred less for Royals; a long-wheelbase chassis was produced for the eight-passenger sedans which Chrysler curiously still kept manufacturing, even when the market for them had almost vanished. A Windsor Six eight-passenger was rather a contradiction in terms.

Through 1952 these six-cylinder models helped Chrysler along at an annual output of 100,000 to 150,000, except in 1950 (when they set a new record of 179,000) and 1952 (when Korean War cutbacks reduced model year production to 87,000). But by the middle fifties Americans had become hooked on V-8s and cars in Chrysler's class were expected to have them. The Division had built a superb new V-8 in the 1951 Hemi, and this engine gradually transformed Chrysler from a manufacturer of reliable but dull cars to reliable and fast ones. Sixes made their last appearance in both Chrysler and DeSoto for 1954, and the Windsor that year ac-

The new generation postwar Chryslers followed K.T. Keller's dictum of practicality over style; this squared-off body was to persist through 1952. From Plymouth to Chrysler the corporate line looked very similar, just larger as one moved up the hierarchy. Oversize taillights with little humps, visible from three sides, and a new version of the "dollar grin" were unique to the Chrysler. This is a '49 Windsor Highlander, upholstered in plaid and leatherette. Highlander interiors were available on coupes and convertibles in Windsor and New Yorker lines, and a few New Yorker sedans.

counted for about 40,000 sales; in 1955, with a new V-8, it racked up nearly 100,000.

Identification

1949: All new boxy styling with simplified egg-crate grille and less overhang front and rear. Town & Country name was used on a wagon for the first time since 1942. Distinctive, all-ways-visible tail-lights with prominent humps on the top of the lens make '49s identifiable at a glance.

1950: Bolder, simpler egg-crate grille, rounded bumpers, taillights fared into rear fenders (or mounted in small vertical housings on wagons).

Wagon tailgates have embossed spare tire outline.

1951: Very simple grille composed of two verti-cal bars with top bar wrapping around to front fender/door moldings. Chrysler name in script on hood; fully-wrapped backlight on closed models.

1952: Same as 1951 but taillight assembly now encompasses back-up lights (one of the few '52 changes on any Chrysler product).

1953: Major facelift created less boxy lines. Three-bar grille with parking lights built into mid-dle bar; taillight/back-up light assembly mounted higher on rear fenders; one-piece curved wind-shield (the first since the Airflow).

The 1950 models had a cleaner front end. These two Royal wagons, the woody and the all-steel ver-sion demonstrate the great leap forward in utility model design that occurred less than a decade after the Town & Country had revolutionized the look of wagons in 1941. From 1951 on, all Town & Countrys would use the sleeker, more durable all-steel body.

This 1951 Windsor Deluxe demonstrates the front and rear facelift which was performed that year: the result was much cleaner lines but no change to the interior. This is almost identical to the '52 Windsor I remember from my youth . . .

More restyling occurred for 1953, when smoother, more rounded styling and a one-piece curved wind-shield came in, while the front end more or less fol-lowed the clean lines of 1951-52. This Windsor Deluxe sedan was the most popular single model in the line, accounting for over 45,000 sales.

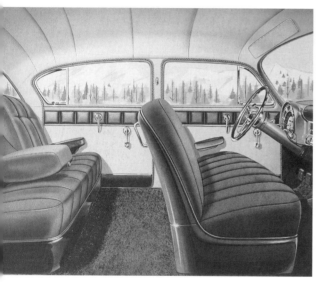

1954: Small central scoop built into grille; parking lights built into headlamp assembly; vertical taillamps "split" by central round back-up lights.

Appraisal

Solid and reliable they may have been, but these Chryslers have excited less collector juices than the heft of postwar production, and the only ones that require a lot of money to buy today are the convertibles, mainly because of their six-million-mile headroom. Conversely, the other models are dirt cheap, quite a lot of them are around with low mileage, and their heavy-duty construction and relative freedom from rust makes for a good survival rate.

Summary and Prospects

Not going anywhere as investment portfolio material; a good buy for the Chrysler devotee not interested in piling up value and not anxious to own a Hemi (if you *are* anxious, see next Chapter).

Return on investment (95-point condition 1):

	1980	1995	*Return
1949 Windsor convertible	$7,000	$20,000	7.3%
1950 Royal station wagon (woody)	$8,600	$18,000	5.0%
1951 Windsor Deluxe club coupe	$2,500	$9,500	9.4%
1952 Windsor Deluxe Newport hardtop	$4,400	$12,500	7.2%
1953 Windsor Deluxe convertible	$6,000	$16,000	6.8%
1954 Windsor Deluxe T&C wagon	$4,500	$13,000	7.4%

*compound annual rate of return unadjusted for maintenance, insurance and running cost

To replace the Saratoga in 1953, Chrysler broke the Windsor Six into standard and deluxe models. What you received for the extra $250 it took to buy a Deluxe is shown by these drawings: the Deluxe had higher quality, pleated upholstery and door panels color keyed to the exterior, while the standard Windsor was very plain. Note also the Deluxe's rear center armrest and chrome assist grips on the seatbacks.

Specifications

Engines (net hp)
Type: cast-iron inline Six with four (1949) or five (1950-54) main bearings.
250.6ci (3.44 x 4.50in), 116hp (1949-50)
264.5ci (3.44 x 4.75in), 119hp (1951-54)

Chassis and Drivetrain
Ladder chassis, shaft drive, four-wheel hydraulic brakes, steel wheels. Fluid Drive transmission with column shift, PowerFlite two-speed automatic optional 1953-54.

Size and Weight
Wheelbase (in):
125.5in; 139.5in (long wheelbase models)
Curb Weight (lb):
Royals, from 3,600lb (sedan) to 4,200 lb (8pass. sedan).
Windsors from 3,700lb (club coupe) to 4,400lb (limousine).

Production

	1949	1950	1951-2	1953	1954
Royal:					
sedan, 4dr.	13,192	17,713	0	0	0
club coupe	4,849	5,900	0	0	0
wagon, 4dr, 9pass., wood	850	599	0	0	0
wagon, 4dr, 9pass., steel	0	100	0	0	0
sedan, 4dr., 8pass.	185	375	0	0	0
Windsor:					
sedan, 4dr.	55,879	78,199	*16,112	18,879	0
Deluxe sedan, 4dr.	0	0	*75,513	45,385	33,563
Traveler sedan, 4dr.	0	900	*850	0	0
club coupe	17,732	20,050	*6,735	11,646	0
Deluxe club coupe	0	0	*8,635	0	5,659
Newport hardtop, 2dr.	0	9,925	*10,200	5,642	3,655
wagon, 4dr., 6pass., steel	0	0	*1,967	1,242	650
convertible	3,234	2,201	*4,200	1,250	500
sedan, 4dr., 8pass.	373	763	*633	425	500
limousine	73	174	*720	0	0
ambulance (special order)	0	0	153	0	0
chassis	0	1	0	0	0

* combined production; approx. breakdown: 1951, 63%; 1952, 37%

The smooth looking 1954 Windsor Deluxe Newport hardtop is a budget collector's item today. The '54s can be told at a glance by their taillights, which moved the back-up lights from the bottom of the assembly to a central position. Kelsey-Hayes chrome wires wheels were an option that really dresses up this model.

★★

Chapter 12

Saratoga & New Yorker
1950-54

The senior Chryslers during the early fifties followed the pattern of the Royal and Windsor: large, high-quality, well-engineered, and solidly built family carriers which lacked any pretense toward high style and thus pleased their creators, notably chairman of the board Keller. It wasn't until Virgil Exner, a young genius with a certain forward look in his eye, arrived at Chrysler Styling that any pretense of fashion crept into renderings and clay models for proposed future Chryslers.

Meanwhile, the New Yorker represented the top of the family car line, while the Saratoga was a detrimmed New Yorker. The redesigned '49s, which debuted in mid-model year, consisted of only five models: a sedan and club coupe for the

Saratoga and New Yorker and a convertible for the latter. A New Yorker Newport hardtop was added in 1950, but though one prototype was built, no senior wagons were offered until 1951: a year which, as history proved, was known for something more exciting than a station wagon. Power steering, a first for Chrysler, was introduced in 1951.

The big news was of course the "Hemi," Chrysler's all-new 331ci V-8, standard for 1951 on all senior models. Though not really a new idea, hemispherical combustion chambers offered exceptionally good volumetric efficiency for truly outstanding performance. The Chrysler Hemi also had a lower compression ratio and could therefore use lower-octane fuel than non-Hemi engines of similar displacement; yet is was capable of producing as much power as a conventional engine with *more* displacement.

The Hemi's output was more than ample: one early demonstration engine achieved 352hp on the dynamometer after minor modifications to the camshaft, carburetors, and exhaust system. Drag

The most important development in Chrysler history since Fluid Drive, the 1951 Hemi-head V-8 brought real performance to the marque for the first time in twenty years.

Extra brightwork and a two-tone top mark this big New Yorker Newport from 1950, the first year for Chrysler hardtops, destined to be major money-earners in time to come. Priced at a hefty $3,200, the Newport still managed to sell nearly 3,000 copies in its freshman year.

racers would later get as much as 1,000hp. On the other hand, the Hemi was complex and costly to build. It required double the number of rocker shafts, pushrods, and rockers; the heads were heavy and expensive. Just eight years later Chrysler would replace it with a wedge-head V-8, but in the meantime it would write history of a kind that Chrysler had not previously experienced.

Despite a reduction in wheelbase for 1951, the New Yorker was too expensive and heavy for heroics. But the relatively light Saratoga was, as an uncle of mine who owned one put it, "Chrysler's hot-rod." A well-tuned Saratoga would do 0-60 in ten seconds and 110mph given enough room. Bill Sterling won the 1951 Mexican Road Race stock car class in a Saratoga, and was third overall, led only by a pair of Ferraris. Chrysler also placed high in stock car racing, though eclipsed in 1952-54 by the Hudson Hornet (an even more unlikely champion). Briggs Cunningham was an early advocate of the Hemi, installing it in his Cunningham sports cars. In 1953, he drove his C-5R to third at the Le Mans Twenty-four Hours, averaging 104.14mph against 105.85 for the winning Jaguar C-type.

Knowing that performance fans would prefer the Saratoga, Chrysler set it on the smaller wheelbase and added a wagon and a longer-wheelbase eight-passenger sedan. They should have added a convertible and a hardtop (one prototype Newport was built), but the appeal of the Hemi transcended even four-door sedans: Saratoga sales leaped from 1,300 the year before to over 28,000. In 1952 horsepower

The New Yorker Newport for 1951 had fresh front end styling and the all-important Hemi-head V-8, but these improvements also cost: it was base-priced at $3,800, a big jump from 1950.

This Saratoga eight-passenger sedan displays the only external change for model year 1952: back-up lights combined with taillights. Only about seventy of these rare Saratogas were produced, and the model was axed for 1953.

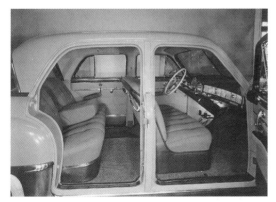

Compare these interiors: the plain vanilla '52 Saratoga and the Highlander Plaid package for the '52 New Yorker. Highlander was usually found only

on sporty models, but did sneak into a handful of sedans. Ordering the Highlander package evidently lost customers the rear center armrest.

A handsome 1953 New Yorker Deluxe convertible, wearing the newly designed '53 body but carrying forward previous themes: integrated taillights and smooth, clean lines. Kelsey-Hayes wires were optional; they add a couple thousand dollars to the value of one today. Only 950 of these ragtops were produced, and they are rare indeed now.

rose to 180, but Korean War cutbacks held production to only about 16,500; New Yorkers sold in about similar quantities both years.

For 1953, a major facelift saw Chrysler reorder its model line-up, with the New Yorker name replacing Saratoga's and the higher priced range rechristened "New Yorker Deluxe," each retaining

The 1954 New Yorker "Le Comte," a show special with a clear plexiglass roof, chrome wires, exterior spare, and special trim, was finished in bronze and black; does any reader know if this one-off has survived?

the 180hp Hemi. The lighter New Yorker appealed to over 40,000 buyers that year. Unfortunately, despite another horsepower increase, the '54s were caught in the midst of the GM-Ford sales wars, and Chrysler lost considerable ground, along with the independents.

Identification

1949: All new boxy styling with simplified egg-crate grille and less overhang front and rear. Distinctive, all-ways-visible taillights with prominent humps on the top of the lens make '49s identifiable at a glance.

1950: Bolder, simpler egg-crate grille, rounded bumpers, taillights fared into rear fenders (or mounted in small vertical housings on wagons). Wagon tailgates have embossed spare tire outline.

1951: Hemi-head V-8 on both Saratoga and New Yorker. Simple grille composed of two vertical bars with top bar wrapping around to front fender/door moldings. Chrysler name in script on hood; fully-wrapped backlight on closed models.

1952: Same as 1951 but taillight assembly now encompasses back-up lights (one of the few '52 changes on any Chrysler product). Broader model range for Saratoga.

1953: Major facelift with Saratoga replaced by New Yorker and New Yorker now called "New Yorker Deluxe." Smoother, less boxy lines. Three-bar grille with parking lights built into middle bar; taillight/back-up light assembly mounted higher on rear fenders; one-piece curved windshield (the first since the Airflow).

1954: Small central scoop built into grille; parking lights built into headlamp assembly; vertical taillamps "split" by central round back-up lights.

Appraisal

From a collector standpoint, Chrysler could have stirred more excitement into the model mix. The early Saratoga is justly famous as the original Hemi, but its most dashing model is the club coupe; what a shame there were no Newports or convertibles. A lightweight Newport did appear in 1953 on the ex-Saratoga New Yorker, but fewer than 4,000 were produced for 1953-54, and there were never any convertibles. Among senior models, these were strictly the province of the New Yorker (1949-52) and New Yorker Deluxe (1953-54). They were produced in very limited quantity, however, and are worth looking for. Newports are also desirable, being handsomely finished with convertible-like materials.

Summary and Prospects

Judged by value increases over the last fifteen years, the model to look for is clearly the 1951-52 Saratoga, with its archetypal hemi-head V-8, a now-

Production

	1949	1950	1951-2	1953	1954
Saratoga:					
sedan, 4dr.	1,810	1,000	*35,516	0	0
club coupe	465	300	*7,847	0	0
Town & Country wagon, 4dr.	0	0	*1,720	0	0
sedan, 4dr., 8passenger***	0	0	*349	0	0
New Yorker (nee Saratoga):					
sedan, 4dr.	0	0	0	37,540	15,788
club coupe	0	0	0	7,749	2,079
Newport hardtop	0	0	0	2,525	1,312
Town & Country wagon, 4dr.	0	0	0	1,399	1,100
sedan, 4dr., 8passenger	0	0	0	100	140
New Yorker (1949-52) / New Yorker Deluxe (1953-54):					
sedan, 4dr.	18,799	22,633	*40,414	20,5852	6,907
club coupe	4,524	3,000	**3,533	1,934	1,861
convertible	1,137	2,800	*2,200	950	724
Newport hardtop	0	0	*5,800	3,715	4,814
chassis	1	2	1	21	17

* combined production; approx. breakdown: 1951, 63%; 1952, 37%
** 1951 model year only
*** In 1951, a limousine with divider window was available on special order and is included in these figures

famous engine that costs a pile more money when found in more recent Chrysler products. I suspect, however, that the Saratoga's admirable appreciation is based more on belated understanding of its role as the first Hemi, or at least the first Hemi in a car weighing less than 4,000 pounds: which is a serious qualifier. It would be interesting to compare the prices over the years of a Saratoga convertible with a New Yorker, but there aren't any of the former. And 1951-52 Saratoga club coupes are worth no more than the same New Yorkers, so the Saratoga's performance edge is not a factor. None of these Chryslers cost a great deal of money; a good condition 3 New Yorker convertible might be had for as little as $12,000, the price of a perfect Saratoga club coupe. But I'd bet my money on a convertible over a club coupe any day.

Return on investment (95-point condition 1):

	1980	1995	*Return
1949-50 New Yorker			
convertible	$7,500	$21,000	7.1%
1949-50 closed models	$4,500	$10,000	5.5%
1951-52 Saratoga			
club coupe	$3,000	$12,500	10.0%
1951-52 New Yorker			
convertible	$7,000	$22,500	8.1%
1952 Saratoga Town			
& Country wagon	$3,900	$19,000	11.2%
1953-54 New Yorker			
Del. convertible	$6,500	$22,500	8.7%
1951-52 New Yorker			
Newport	$4,000	$16,000	9.7%

	1980	1995	*Return
1953-54 New Yorker			
Newport	$5,000	$20,000	9.7%
1953-54 New Yorker			
sedan/coupe	$2,600	$10,000	9.4%

*compound annual rate of return unadjusted for maintenance, insurance, and running costs

---

Specifications

Engines (net hp)
Type: cast-iron inline Eight with five main bearings (1949-50)
Hemi-head V-8 (1951-54)
323.5ci (3.25 x 4.88in), 135hp (1949-50)
331.1ci (3.81 x 3.63in), 180hp (1951-53), 235hp (1954)

Chassis and Drivetrain
Ladder chassis, shaft drive, four-wheel hydraulic brakes, steel wheels. Fluid Drive transmission with column shift, PowerFlite two-speed automatic optional 1953, standard 1954.

Size and Weight
Wheelbase (in):
131.5in (1949-50, 1951-52 New Yorker); 125.5in (1951-52 New Yorker, all 1953-54 models); 139.5in (1951-54 eight-passenger sedan)
Curb Weight (lb):
3,900-4,000lb (Saratoga and 1953-54 New Yorker); 4,000-4,400lb (1949-52 New Yorker, 1953-54 New Yorker Deluxe).

Chapter 13

Imperial & Crown Imperial
1950-54

Commencing with the new postwar styling of mid-1949, the Imperial line of owner-driver luxury sedans reappeared for the first time in a decade, though not very auspiciously: only fifty examples of the close-to-$5,000 Imperial sedan were built. Its low sales were due not only to price, but to availability. Each Imperial was custom-finished by Ray Dietrich in Grand Rapids, Michigan, who painted them in lacquer and fitted them with a special interior and an upholstered Haartz top with a small oval rear window. This meant painfully limited production. Perhaps another reason for their low appeal was that the cars didn't actually say "Imperial" but retained the New Yorker nameplates and "Chrysler" hubcaps.

Derham, the old-line custom bodyworks in Rosemont, Pennsylvania, produced these handsome formal limousines on the Crown Imperial chassis for special Chrysler dealer order in 1950. To the conventional steel roof, Derham added a padded leather top and a small oval rear window with "formal" or "blind" rear quarters. Stylewise these Derhams appear very nicely proportioned: the more you stretch it out, the better K. T. Keller's boxy shape looks!

For 1950 Chrysler distinguished the Imperial with special touches like a wrapped backlight similar to the Newport hardtop's and Imperial badging. They also drastically lowered the price, which started around $3,000, and the result was over 10,000 sales. For 1951, in addition to the new Hemi V-8, the Imperial line featured a club coupe, Newport hardtop, and a convertible, the latter being the first Imperial ragtop since the war (and the only one until 1957).

Through 1952, Imperials were mounted on the New Yorker chassis, but in 1953, when the New Yorker wheelbase was shared with the Windsor, the Imperial received its own, much longer wheelbase and still more distinctive styling: a heavier grille than other Chryslers, a sloping hood; and a curious, downward perched eagle mascot. The '53 and its similar '54 successor were called "Custom Imperials," though the Imperial name alone appeared on the cars. A six-passenger "town limousine" (sedan with divider windows) was offered in both years, but a convertible never materialized, though at least one prototype was built.

The long-wheelbase Crown Imperial followed the same styling evolution from 1949 to 1954, retaining its own 145.5in wheelbase, and was available in eight-passenger sedan or limousine (sedan with divider window) form for all six model years. Production never exceeded 500 per year and was often much less: a mere 100, for example, in 1954 when corporate sales skidded generally. The Crown had never been able to crack Cadillac's stranglehold on the executive car market, though Chrysler's success with the revived owner-driver Imperials prompted the corporation to bill Imperial as a separate make in 1955.

Identification

1949: All new boxy styling with simplified egg-crate grille and less overhang front and rear. Standard Chrysler all-ways-visible taillights were on the Imperial Derham sedan only; other Imperials carried smaller, bulging taillights mounted lower on the fenders. Crown Imperial on longer wheelbase with center-opening doors.

1950: Bolder, simpler egg-crate grille, rounded bumpers. Except on the Imperial, taillights fared into rear fenders (or mounted in small vertical housings on wagons). Newport-style wrapped backlight on sedan models.

1951: Distinctive grille, simpler than other Chryslers, looking like a one-piece unit with prominent "V" and crown emblem, crown medallion hood ornament, and Imperial script on front of hood. Skirted rear wheel openings, no bodyside brightwork, except along rocker panels and lower

part of skirt through rear fender. "Imperial" script on front fenders, hood, and deck. Imperial serial numbers 7736501 to 7753512.

1952: Same as 1951 (unlike other Chryslers, the taillight design did not change); power steering standard. Quickest ID is through serial numbers, which ran from 7753601 to 7763596.

1953: Major facelift with less boxy lines. New eagle hood ornament. One-piece curved windshield. Back-up lights mounted in center of taillights. Crown Imperial similar on longer wheelbase,

The 1949 Crown Imperial limousine, wearing new styling, was a rare breed in its first year only forty-five being produced (along with forty long-wheelbase sedans). The cars are extremely rare today.

Imperial, progressing further to the "owner-driver" concept, brought out its first Newport hardtop for 1951, building about 750 for the model year. The body was still undoubtedly of Chrysler origins, but special badging, bumpers fender skirts, and taillights, plus a posh interior, helped set it apart.

Beautifully smooth and uncluttered, the mid-year 1953 Imperial Newport cost close to $5,000 yet managed nearly 900 sales. Smooth on the highway, and fast thanks to its 180hp Hemi, this was a cleanly styled car in an age of excess: a nice one to own today.

The hefty Crown Imperial sold for $5,300 and earned 100 sales in 1954. The drooping-eagle mascot was a feature of both 1953 and 1954 Imperials. This was a competitive product with its smooth V-8 and ample luxury, but Cadillac owned the professional car market.

A unique Imperial showcar, "La Comtesse" was finished in pink and white, carried a clear Plexiglas roof and a custom interior along with wire wheels and "continental" spare tire. Its counterpart was the New Yorker "Le Comte," a similar confection in black and bronze.

with distinctive moldings on tops of rear fenders of limousines. Newport arrived late in model year, the first Chrysler car with Powerflite automatic.

1954: Single bar, cheap-looking Chevy-like grille with five ridges and built-in circular parking lights. Back-up lights mounted below taillights. Eagle hood ornament unchanged.

Appraisal

The most expensive of all Chryslers from the early fifties, owner-driver Imperials offer elaborate trim and high luxury to collectors; performance is considerably enhanced on 1951 and later models through the new Hemi V-8. The 1951-only convertible is highly desirable, followed by Newport hardtops, which were offered in all years except 1949-50. The big Crown Imperials are of interest chiefly to "professional car" collectors. All models are extremely well built and relatively impervious to rust. Produced in small quantities, with small but distinctive styling differences to the other Chryslers, Imperials are well worth the time of marque specialists and general collectors interested in some-

thing different. The Derham sedan of 1949 is particularly rare and desirable.

Summary and Prospects

Considering that they only made 650 and only in one model year from the end of the war through 1957, the '51 Imperial convertible almost is underpriced. But this seems one case where low supply is nullified by relatively low demand—there's much more collector interest in the flashier, bigger, more powerful Imperial convertibles of the late fifties. Considering that a very good, 80+ point '51 ought not to cost more than the price of a new Hyundai, this early open Imperial is a good buy, and stands to appreciate more rapidly in the next fifteen years than the last fifteen.

Among the next-most-desirable Newport hardtops, there is quite a difference in value between the upright, boxy 1951-52 generation and the smoother, more modern 1953-54 models; the '54 with its 235hp Hemi is particularly recommended. Crown Imperials have appreciated in value right along with the owner-driver models,

Production

	1949	1950	1951-2	1953	1954
Imperial:					
sedan, 4dr.	0	9,500	*21,711	7,793	4,324
Deluxe sedan, 4dr.	**50	1,150	0	0	0
club coupe	0	0	*3,533	0	0
Newport hardtop	0	0	*1,189	823	1,249
convertible	0	0	***650	0	0
Town Limousine, 6pass.	0	0	0	243	85
Crown Imperial:					
sedan, 4dr., 8pass.	40	209	*360	48	23
limo, 8pass.	45	205	*338	111	77
chassis	0	1	2	1	0

* combined production; approx. breakdown: 1951, 63%; 1952, 37%
** custom by Dietrich
*** 1951 model year only
Note: Three 1954 Imperial chassis were also built, one carrying a prototype convertible.

though space is a problem to consider before acquiring one of these behemoths.

Return on investment (95-point condition 1):

	1980	1995	*Return
1949 sedan by Dietrich	$4,100	$13,000	8.0%
1950-54 sedan, 4dr.	$3,000	$10,000	8.4%
1949-54 Crown Imperial limousine	$5,000	$16,000	8.1%
1951 convertible	$7,000	$21,000	7.6%
1951-52 Newport hardtop	$5,700	$15,000	6.7%
1953-54 Newport hardtop	$6,500	$22,500	8.7%

*compound annual rate of return unadjusted for maintenance, insurance, and running costs

Specifications
Engines (net hp)
Type: cast-iron inline 8 (1949-50) and hemi-head V-8 (1951-54)
323.5ci (3.25 x 4.88in), 135hp (1949-50)
331.1ci (3.81 x 3.63in), 180hp (1951-53), 235hp (1954)

Chassis and Drivetrain
Ladder chassis, shaft drive, four-wheel hydraulic brakes, steel wheels. Fluid Drive transmission with column shift through mid-1953, PowerFlite two-speed automatic standard, mid-1953 and 1954.

Size and Weight
Wheelbase (in):
131.5in (1949-52 Imperial, 1953 Imperial Newport), 133.5in (1953-54 Imperial), 145.5in (Crown Imperial)
Curb Weight (lb):
1949-54 Imperial 4,300-4,400lb; 1951 Imperial convertible 4,570lb; Crown Imperials about 5,300lb.

The town limousine was a 123.5in-wheelbase compact professional car designed for use in cities; it was fairly successful in 1953 but these '54 models sold sparingly. This one carries Chrysler Airtemp air conditioning: note scoops on rear fenders. A heavy bright metal trim strip around the side windows, with a stylized "I" and crown symbol, were special features of the town limo.

Chapter 14

Windsor, Saratoga, & Newport
1955-61

The story of what Chrysler called the "Hundred Million Dollar Look" is, obviously, one of styling; and the author of that styling, Virgil Exner, became, almost overnight, a household word—like Raymond Loewy before him. It must have been sweet triumph for Exner, whom Loewy had fired from his Studebaker design team when Exner began moonlighting to compete with the team's own designs. The '55 corporate line was entirely styled under Exner, and there wasn't a dull car in it.

The Chryslers, Imperials, and DeSotos were inspired by Exner's 1952 Imperial Parade Phaetons, huge showcars on a long wheelbase, which were later reworked with 1955-56 Imperial front ends and rear sheet metal. Chrysler had its own look, distinct from Imperial: huge "twin tower" taillights defined the back end, and a pair of small eggcrate grilles up front, surmounting a horizontal car containing the parking lights. Two-toning was now the rage: on the baseline Windsor Deluxe (the word "Deluxe" was dropped in 1956) it usually consisted of the hood, roof, and upper part of the body back to the "C" pillar finished in a contrasting color. Some cars were simply two-toned on the roof, while there were vari-

ations, such as the special Newport hardtops and sedans for Spring 1955 (see Identification), with the contrast color spread over the deck and running forward in a spear along the fenders. The body line-up consisted of a sedan, convertible, two hardtop coupes, and a Town & Country wagon.

In addition to assigning Exner chief responsibility for styling, President Tex Colbert dropped the Six from all his senior makes, calling it "as dead as a dodo." The baseline Windsor did not receive a Hemi; its powerplant was a very good 300ci polyspherical head unit with the intake and exhaust valves placed diagonally across from each other rather than directly opposite as in the Hemi. This allowed a single rocker shaft for each bank of cylinders, making spark plugs more accessible. Poly-heads weighed less than hemi-heads and the engine was much less costly to build; yet it retained most of the Hemi's desirable breathing qualities. Windsors used the smaller Hemi engine for 1956-58.

Chrysler came back with a slightly facelifted, tailfinned '56 model, and added a new body style, the Newport four-door hardtop. Most models

The two trim versions of 1955 Windsor hardtops. The plainer Nassau was two-toned on the roof only, while the Newport, which cost $105 more, had flashy deck/body side two-toning which was sometimes also applied to the roof, and slightly more deluxe trim including a bright metal panel on the rear roof quarters. Newport is the rarer car but there's little difference in value.

A handsome restyle, the '56 Windsor featured Exner's first tailfins and a more integrated, single-section grille of horizontal bars. Production was down and scarcely 1,000 of these $3,500 convertibles were sold.

now had PowerFlite two-speed automatic transmission, which had arrived in 1953, though Windsors could technically be ordered with three-speed manual transmission. In 1957 PowerFlite was joined by three-speed TorqueFlite. All automatics adopted pushbutton controls starting in 1956. Sales of '56s were well down compared to the '55s, which had held Chrysler ahead of Cadillac in ninth place in the sales race—a position it would not again achieve for many years. The Saratoga returned for 1957, and over 37,000 were sold that year. Although now more closely related to the Windsor than the New Yorker, the Saratoga still offered high performance through a more powerful engine, a 295hp version of the Hemi, in a lighter body than the New Yorker. The '57s, which ushered in Exner's smoothly finned, cleanly styled "Forward Look," were the swoopiest cars in their class. Chrysler Corporation was now the acknowledged Detroit styling leader. While styling was superb, Chrysler's rush to set the pace had a negative effect on overall quality. Workmanship was also hampered by a series of strikes.

The engineering news for 1957 was Torsion-Aire ride (torsion bar front suspension), which made Chrysler products the best handling fullsize cars in the industry. Instead of sending road shocks up into the car like coil or leaf springs, torsion bars absorbed force by winding up against their anchor points. The resultant twisting motion eliminated most of the upward force caused by road irregularities.

Partly as a result of buyer unhappiness with 1957 quality control, and partly because of a reces-

Four-door hardtops entered the field in 1956; with 1957's new "Forward Look" styling they appeared especially sleek; color panel for bodysides was optional. Unprecedented glass area and clean lines were a Chrysler styling trademark this year, but the cars suffered from early rust-out.

sion, 1958 was a terrible year for Chrysler. There was no major styling change to enhance the line's allure although the '58 Windsor was a much different car, cutting heavily into DeSoto territory. Higher hopes were pinned on Exner's 1959 restyle, a less graceful affair with soaring tailfins. The "Lion-Hearted" 1959 Chrysler scored close to 70,000 sales for the model year.

After a two-year absence of junior convertibles, a softtop Windsor was added in 1959, but otherwise the '59 line stayed the same: Windsors rode a 122in wheelbase that had appeared the year before, while Saratoga's kept the 126in wheelbase that had been

Pushbuttons were all the rage by 1958, as shown on this Windsor convertible's dashboard; they controlled the TorqueFlite automatic (left) and heating controls (right, under wheel) as well as the radio. The rearview mirror's position suggests the lowness of the car.

A 1958 Windsor four-door hardtop with mid-year "Dartline" side trim, still very clean, but the taillights had curiously shrunk, filling up only half of the space provided for them in the tailfins.

used since 1955. Both models carried the new wedge-head V-8, not as powerful as the Hemi but simpler to build. A novel option was swivel front seats that pivoted outward through a latch. For 1960, the seats swiveled when the doors were opened.

During the early sixties, advertising stridently proclaimed that there would never be a small Chrysler: a promise, as time proved, impossible to keep. For the moment, they meant it: the 1960-61 Chryslers were Exner's last outlandishly plumed creations. In the vernacular of the stylist they were clean, uncluttered by excess chrome, fitted with acres of glass and aggressive, trapezoid grillework. Detail improvements for 1960 included four-way hazard flashers. Most importantly, Chrysler adopted a unit chassis-body for 1960, designed to minimize noise and improve solidity; unfortunately, it was no less susceptible to rust than the 1957-59 separate body.

The Saratoga had its last year in 1960. The Windsor lasted through 1961, when its ultimate successor appeared. This was the Newport, taking up a name previously applied to hardtop models. Downpriced some $300 from the Windsor, running a slightly smaller V-8, and offering a full line including a convertible and six- or nine-passenger wagons, the Newport was a popular medium priced car. Its arrival signaled not only the end of the long-running Windsor but of the entire DeSoto range, since it competed smack against DeSoto and had the advantage of Chrysler's more upmarket badge.

Identification

1955: Tall, narrow, "Twin-Tower" taillamps in large chromium housings; divided egg-crate grille; round parking lights set in fenders underneath headlamps. Dashboard mounted shift lever. Two two-door hardtops were offered: Nassau, more conservatively trimmed; and Newport, with better trim, usually two-toned, priced about $115 higher. "Spring Specials" were the Newport "Green Falcon" and "Blue Heron," green and blue color schemes similar in pattern to the New Yorker St. Regis, with color keyed interiors. Nassau and Newport may be differentiated at a glance by the name applied to their "C" pillars.

1956: Rear tailfins with tall, integrated taillights; oblong grille of horizontal bars flanked by rectangular parking lamps. The Nassau/Newport trim options continued for two-door hardtops, but a four-door Newport hardtop was added. Pushbutton automatic featured for the first time. "Deluxe" omitted from Windsor model name.

1957: All-new styling with smooth, tall tailfins housing huge integrated taillights; full-width inverted trapezoidal grille. Two-toned Windsors offered a color flash in the contrasting (roof) color on the sides of rear fenders; Saratogas carried a single, full-length bright bodyside molding and optional color sweep. Quad headlamps were optional. Dome-like, wrapover windshield on convertibles.

1958: Styling similar 1957, quickly identifiable by "shrunken" taillights which did not fill the backs of the rear fenders as they had in 1957. Windsor rode a smaller, 122in wheelbase. Windsor Dartline trim package for hardtops consisted of extra front fender trim with metal insert, bright sill moldings, special roof trim and three slim moldings on each side of rear license plate receptacle. Saratoga retained 126in wheelbase. Quad headlamps standard.

1959: A facelift with rounded eyebrows over quad headlamps, horizontal grille wrapping around at sides of front fenders, more massive bumpers; rear license plate mounted in bumper instead of deck. Dome-like windshield now found on hardtops as well as convertibles. Optional on hardtops was an "outlined roof" with its edges painted in the same contrasting color as the sidespear. Sweepspear was "bent" at mid-body on Windsor; on Saratoga it ran straight back from the front, dipping low on the rear fenders.

1960: All new styling with canted tailfins carrying fared-in, curved taillamps; trapezoidal grille composed of egg-crate mesh and lion emblem in center. Saratoga identified by model name script and longer front overhand, as well as fancier interior and longer wheelbase.

1961: Last of the tailfinned Chryslers: canted quad headlamps, taillamps relocated in horizontal housings under the tailfins. Inverted trapezoid grille with prominent horizontal bars. Saratoga dropped and Windsor reduced to three body styles. Newport was the new series.

Appraisal

Within this group of junior Chryslers are some of the most collectible examples of the marque. Commencing in 1955, Chrysler added high style to its already respected engineering prowess; from 1957 Chrysler styling "led the league," though its lead was temporary, and was again eclipsed by GM in the early sixties. High-output Hemi engines, colorful (if not very durable) interiors, torsion-bar front suspension and unique options like swivel seats and Highway Hi-Fi (the semi-successful optional record player, requiring special records to avoid groove-bounce) are period fixtures which attract collectors. Convertibles were beautiful boats; hardtops were equally sleek; and there's a plentiful supply of cars to choose from.

A heavy facelift produced a less distinctive Chrysler Windsor in 1959, but there was more power, with the 305hp Golden Lion 383, a long-lived and reliable V-8. Stylists were now experimenting with novel two-tone patterns as shown on this car's roof, veering away from heavy bodyside two-toning.

The long, tapered profile of the 1960 Windsor two-door hardtop reflected the height of Virgil Exner's tailfin styling era. This was the last year for a full range of Windsor body styles; in 1961 its bottom-of-the-line position was held by the Newport and in 1963 it was dropped altogether.

Highlander Plaid, a Chrysler upholstery pattern that started in 1941, was available on the mid-year 1961 Newport, whose "high back" driver's seat prefigured modern headrests. It's surprising that the plaid pattern wasn't more popular; surviving examples are rare today.

Specifications

Engines (net hp)
Type: cast-iron V-8, poly-head (1955 Windsor Deluxe), hemi-head (1956-58), wedge-head (1959-61)
301.0ci (3.63 x 3.63 in.), 188hp (1955 Windsor Deluxe)
331.1ci (3.81 x 3.63 in.), 225hp, 250hp optional (1956 Windsor)
331.1ci (3.81 x 3.63 in.), 285/290hp (1957-58 Windsor)
331.1ci (3.81 x 3.63 in.), 295/310hp (1957-58 Saratoga)
383.0ci (4.03 x 3.75 in.), 305hp (1959-61 Windsor)
383.0ci (4.03 x 3.75 in.), 325hp (1959-60 Saratoga)
261.0ci (4.12 x 3.38 in.), 265hp (1961 Newport)

Chassis and Drivetrain
Separate chassis frame (1955-59) unit body and frame (1960-61); shaft drive, four-wheel hydraulic brakes, steel wheels. Three-speed manual transmission standard on Windsor and 1961 Newport, PowerFlite (1955-56) and TorqueFlite (1956-61) optional. TorqueFlite standard on Saratoga.

Size and Weight
Wheelbase (in):
126in (1955-57, 1958-60 Saratoga); 122in (1958-61 Windsor and 1961 Newport)
Curb Weight (lb):
1955-59 Windsor 3,850-4,000lb, wagons 4,100-4,300lb; 1957-59 Saratoga 4,000-4,300lb Unibody models; 1960-61 Windsor 3,700-3,850lb, wagons 4,250-4,400lb; 1961 Newport 3,700-3,800lb, wagons 4,100-4,200lb

---

Among all corporate makes, Chrysler probably offered the smoothest, most unified styling, wearing its big tailfins with grace (at least in 1956-58). Do note, however, that rust is a severe problem beginning with the 1957 models, and even harder to deal with on the unit bodies which began in 1960.

Summary and Prospects

This group of Chryslers comprises an attractive collector prospect, and has appreciated rapidly over the past fifteen years. Of course the chief gains in value will be among convertibles and two-door hardtops, but the sedans are almost dirt cheap, and a nice '55 is certainly desirable. There is a wide range of price scales to choose from: you can still buy quite a good Newport convertible for under five figures: even a perfect one should not cost you more than $12,000, though the asking price may be higher than that. Whether these mass-volume models represent as good a buy today as the limited edition 300 (Chapter 16) may be judged by their comparative gains in value over the past decade or so. This is no guarantee of their performance in the future, but it gives some inkling of their prospects, assuming no drastic economic upheavals. As a group: strongly recommended.

Return on investment (95-point condition 1):

	1980	1995	*Return
1955 Windsor convertible	$6,000	$24,000	9.7%
1956-58 Windsor 2dr. hardtop	$3,900	$17,500	10.6%
1957-59 Saratoga 2dr. hardtop	$3,000	$20,000	11.4%
1959-60 Windsor convertible	$4,000	$18,000	10.6%
1955-61 sedans & wagons (all)	$2,500	$7,000	7.1%
1956-61 4dr. hardtops (all)	$2,750	$11,000	9.7%
1961 Newport convertible	$3,800	$12,000	8.0%

*compound annual rate of return unadjusted for maintenance, insurance, and running costs

One more time for the tailfinned Chrysler: the mildly facelifted '61 Newport convertible, which sold for $3,500 but saw only a couple thousand sales.

Production

	1955	1956	1957	1958	1959
Windsor (Windsor Deluxe in 1955):					
sedan, 4dr.	63,896	53,119	17,639	12,861	19,910
hardtop, 4dr.	0	7,050	14,354	6,254	6,084
Nassau hardtop, 2dr.	18,474	11,400	0	0	0
Newport hardtop, 2dr.	13,126	10,800	0	0	0
hardtop, 2dr.	0	0	14,027	6,205	6,775
convertible	1,395	1,011	0	0	961
Town & Country wagon	1,983	2,700	2,035	1,453	1,743
Saratoga:					
sedan, 4dr.	0	0	14,977	8,698	8,783
hardtop, 4dr.	0	0	11,586	5,322	4,943
hardtop, 2dr.	0	0	10,633	4,466	3,753

	1960	1961
Windsor:		
sedan, 4dr.	25,152	10,239
hardtop, 4dr.	5,897	4,156
hardtop, 2dr.	6,496	2,941
convertible	1,467	0
Town & Country wagon	2,146	0
Saratoga:		
sedan, 4dr.	8,463	0
hardtop, 4dr.	4,099	0
hardtop, 2dr.	2,963	0
Newport:		
sedan, 4dr.	0	34,370
hardtop, 4dr.	0	7,789
hardtop, 2dr.	0	9,405
convertible	0	2,135
Town & Country wagon	0	2,403

Chapter 15

New Yorker
1955-61

A significant step up the ladder in price from the Windsor, Saratoga, and Newport was the Chrysler New Yorker ("New Yorker Deluxe" in 1955), produced throughout this period on a uniform 126in wheelbase and offering greater luxury inside, flashier trim outside and the most powerful V-8s short of the limited edition 300 at commensurately higher prices. In 1955, a New Yorker sedan ($3,500 base price) cost nearly $900 more than a base Windsor; by 1961, when Chrysler purposely base-priced the Newport at just under $3,000, a New Yorker sedan started at $4,123.

There were several two-tone (and in 1956 three-tone) color schemes, the most common of which was a dart-shaped color panel running along the body sides matching the color on the roof. Like the Windsor, there were two grades of two-door hardtops in 1955-56: the plainer Newport and the up-market St. Regis, although the price differential between them was only $30, not $115 as on the Wind-

sor. On two-tone St. Regis models, the second (roof) color was applied to the hood and along the tops of the fenders and doors and back to the "C" pillar. A "Summer Special" combined this treatment with the standard New Yorker color panel on four-door sedans and Newport hardtops; it cost only $8.60 extra and about 2,000 such packages were sold: 12 percent of production, which means there must be a few survivors.

Nineteen fifty-six brought a restyled New Yorker with handsome tailfins encompassing smooth integrated tail/back-up lights, and a new four-door hardtop (Newport). Two-tone patterns now resembled those of the 1955 St. Regis. All-new "Forward Look" styling and Torsion-Aire Ride marked the sleek '57s, which saw price increases up to $600 as the New Yorker was moved further up-market. This was also the first year horsepower exceeded 300 on a standard Chrysler. The 1958s were a repeat of the '57s but are much scarcer today because they

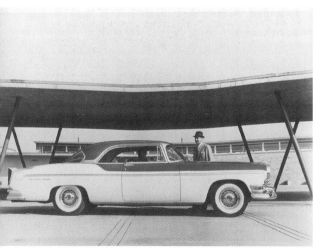

The New Yorker St. Regis hardtop outsold the plainer Newport version by about two to one and looked very sporty indeed with optional wire wheels and hedonistic two-toning.

At $4,200 the New Yorker Town & Country wagon was the most expensive model in the 1955 line, more even than the 300. Note the early taillight housings, which were truncated to fit the wagon fenders; later wagons had regular taillights.

Three-tone styling was featured on the 1956 New Yorker hardtop, which was often shown in this combination of red, white, and black. Hashmarks on rear fenders are an instant identity mark; a 280hp Hemi was under the hood.

didn't sell nearly as well. The '59s, with more rounded front ends but the familiar, sharply peaked tailfin rear fenders, came with new wedge-head V-8s of 413ci: a sound, reliable "big-block" destined to live a long corporate life.

Unibody construction and flared out tailfins followed typical 1960 styling hallmarks, but New Yorkers were always easily told at a glance by their extra trim and badging, or other special details, including a recessed grille. In 1961 it was the grille, which had vertical and horizontal bars, making it look more elaborate than the horizontal-barred Newport and Windsor.

Throughout this period the New Yorker retained a consistent line of popular body styles: sedans, hardtops (with four doors as well as two beginning 1956), convertibles, and Town & Country wagons (sold with and without a third seat, giving nine-passenger capacity, from 1958). What changed was their volume. The New Yorker had started out at about $3,500 in 1955, when it sold over 50,000 copies, 60 percent of the Windsor level. By 1960 it was typically priced over $5,000, and that year fewer than 18,000 were sold, 30 percent of the Windsor/Saratoga level. Chrysler cut prices for 1961, when the New Yorker sedan came in at just over $4,000, but sales were almost identical to 1960. In addition to its accelerating pricetag, changing public tastes had seen a sales decline among big, upper-medium priced cars like this, and one day within twenty years a very small Chrysler indeed would bear the distinguished New Yorker nameplate.

Identification

1955: Tall, narrow, "Twin-Tower" taillamps in large chromium housings with horizontal chrome bars on lenses; divided egg-crate grille surmount-

The face of Chrysler, 1957, the peak year for the "Forward Look." Wide fender openings housed quad headlamps on some models; they were standard in 1958. Smooth lines and elegant horizontal grille expressed the best of the Virgil Exner design philosophy. This is a magnificent looking New Yorker.

ing a single bar with oval parking lights in extremities (the theme was repeated on the rear back-up lights). Dashboard mounted shift lever. Two two-door hardtops were offered: Newport, more conservatively trimmed; and St. Regis with better trim, usually two-toned, $30 higher. "Summer Special" was a Newport or sedan wearing both St. Regis trim and a two-tone color flash. Small nameplates at base of "C" pillar identify Newport and St. Regis.

1956: Rear tailfins with tall, integrated taillights; oblong grille of many fine horizontal and vertical bars flanked by rectangular parking lamps and wing-edged front bumpers. The Newport/St. Regis trim options continued for two-door hardtops, but a four-door Newport hardtop was added. Pushbutton automatic featured for the first time. "Deluxe" omitted from New Yorker model name. First hallmark "hashmarks" on rear fender.

1957: All-new styling with smooth, tall tailfins housing huge integrated taillights; full-width inverted trapezoidal grille. Two-toned New Yorkers carried a color flash in the contrasting (roof) color on a slim, dart-shaped body panel similar to but thinner than 1955. Six vertical chrome flashes on each rear fender. Quad headlamps were optional. Dome-like, wrapover windshield on convertibles.

1958: Styling similar to 1957, quickly identifiable by "shrunken" taillights which did not fill the backs of the rear fenders as they had in 1957. Bodyside trim was now a chrome molding starting at rear door, widening to an anodized panel with a small emblem on rear doors or fenders; six vertical hash marks remained on rear fenders. Quad headlamps standard.

1959: A facelift with rounded eyebrows over quad headlamps, horizontal grille wrapping around at sides of front fenders, more massive bumpers; rear license plate mounted in bumper instead of deck. Taillights carried high in rear fender peaks. Golden lion mounted with New Yorker script on front fenders. Dome-like windshield now found on hardtops as well as convertibles. Optional on hardtops was an "outlined roof" with its edges painted in contrasting color. Bodyside trim was a spear running front to rear, with seven hashmarks contained within an anodized aluminum panel it at the rear.

1960: Unibody construction. New styling with canted tailfins carrying fared-in, curved taillamps; frenched (inset) trapezoidal grille composed of fine

As typically encountered, the 1957 New Yorker hardtop, this one fitted with optional quad headlamps. As clean a piece of fifties styling as Detroit ever put together, this is a classic work of Exner art. About 9,000 were built and a few are occasionally advertised.

For 1958 the taillights shrank but little else was changed; two-toning for Saratoga was unique, somewhat plainer than New Yorker. Fewer than 5,000 Saratoga two-door hardtops left the factory.

The 1958 New Yorker convertible, little changed from 1957, can be identified by its special body side trim and new style wheel covers. With a recession on, sales were low, and convertible sales extremely so; thus we are looking at a very rare car, one of only 666 built.

A bolder and busier look attended the 1959 New Yorker, which topped $5,000 as typically equipped. Designers had now wrapped the windshield of closed models around at the top as well at the sides; this had been seen on convertibles earlier.

Substantially restyled, the 1960 New Yorker offered more interior space than before, retained the big 413ci wedge-head V-8 with 350 horsepower. Tail-lights were neatly integrated into the fins and traditional hashmarks survived on lower rear fenders.

horizontal bars and lion emblem in center. Hashmarks on lower rear fenders as before, but now nine in number.

1961: Last of the tailfinned Chryslers: canted quad headlamps, taillamps relocated in horizontal housings under the tailfins and back-up lamps set into chrome housings at the tops of the fins. Wagons used 1960 style rear fenders. Inverted trapezoid grille with vertical and horizontal bars.

Appraisal

Sold at far higher prices than the Windsor, Saratoga, or Newport, the New Yorker is the choice of collectors for whom luxury is important, although performance is hardly dull, since New Yorkers almost always had more powerful engines. Stylewise the '57 is the purest example of Virgil Exner's concepts, though the 1955-56 models are better built. Three-speed TorqueFlite automatic with pushbutton controls, which arrived in mid-1956, is a better transmission than PowerFlite and more likely to be familiar to mechanics. Convertibles are extremely rare and easily the most desirable models. Rust is a severe problem beginning with the 1957 models, and even harder to deal with on the unit bodies which began in 1960.

Summary and Prospects

It is interesting to compare the relative values of top-condition New Yorkers to their junior counterparts in the same years (previous chapter). Convertibles have run about the same with the startling exception of the 1957-59 models,

A domed dashboard with advanced electro-luminescent lighting flanked by automatic and heater/air conditioning pushbuttons was part of the 1960-61 styling series, here seen on an unfinished Saratoga.

where the New Yorkers have appreciated 50 percent faster than the Windsors. The 1957-58 New Yorker two-door hardtop, which sold for a paltry $2,900 in top condition in 1980, has appreciated faster than any Chrysler covered to this point, returning nearly fifteen percent on your money if you bought a show-quality car in 1980. Sedans and wagons have gained in value at the same pace whether they are Windsors, Saratogas, or New Yorkers, but the 1956-59 New Yorker four-door hardtop has risen at a much faster rate than the Windsor or Saratoga.

The '61 wagons retained 1960-style rear ends with integrated taillights. Cross-hatched New Yorker grille was clearly up-market from the Windsor and Newport. Town & Country wagons cost about $5,000 as usually equipped and weighed close to two tons.

Specifications
Engines (net hp)
Type: cast-iron V-8, hemi-head (1956-58), wedge-head (1959-61)
331.1ci (3.81 x 3.63in), 250hp (1955), 280hp (1956)
392.0ci (4.00 x 3.90in), 325hp (1957), 345hp (1958)
413.0ci (4.18 x 3.75in), 350hp (1959-61)

Chassis and Drivetrain
Separate chassis frame (1955-59) unit body and frame (1960-61); shaft drive, four-wheel hydraulic brakes, steel wheels. Automatic transmission standard (PowerFlite 1955-56, TorqueFlite 1956-61).

Size and Weight
Wheelbase (in):
126in
Curb Weight (lb):
1955-58 4,200lb, convertibles 4,300lb, wagons 4,450lb; 1959 4,100-4,300lb, wagons 4,300-4,400lb Unit body chassis: 1960-61 4,200lb, wagons 4,520lb

The advice we can draw from all these statistics is that the beautifully styled 1957-58 New Yorker is a "best buy" in convertible or hardtop form, and that the later 1960-61 models are moving much slower on the collector market, with the '59s in between. Among convertibles, the sleek '57/'58s are now worth more than the handsome '55/'56s—it was the other way around fifteen years ago.

Return on investment (95-point condition 1):

	1980	1995	*Return
1955-56 convertible	$6,500	$30,000	10.8%
1955-56 2dr. hardtop	$4,750	$21,000	10.5%
1957-58 2dr. hardtop	$2,900	$23,000	14.9%
1957-59 convertible	$4,900	$32,000	13.4%
1960-61 convertible	$4,000	$15,000	9.3%
1955-61 sedans & wagons	$2,500	$7,500	7.6%
1956-59 4dr. hardtops	$2,750	$13,000	11.0%
1960-61 4dr. hardtops	$2,500	$8,000	8.1%

*compound annual rate of return unadjusted for maintenance, insurance, and running costs

Production

	1955	1956	1957	1958	1959
sedan, 4dr.	33,342	24,749	12,369	7,110	7,792
hardtop, 4dr.	0	3,599	10,948	5,227	4,805
St. Regis hardtop, 2dr.	11,076	6,686	0	0	0
Newport hardtop, 2dr.	5,777	4,115	0	0	0
hardtop, 2dr.	0	0	8,863	3,205	2,434
convertible	946	921	1,049	666	286
Town & Country wagon	1,036	1,070	1,391	1,203	1,008

	1960	1961
sedan, 4dr.	9,079	9,984
hardtop, 4dr.	5,625	5,862
hardtop, 2dr.	2,835	2,541
convertible	556	576
Town & Country wagon	1,295	1,436

Chapter 16

300 Letter Series
1955-65

The first of what we now call "muscle cars" swept the stock car racing boards clean and built a following much larger than there were cars to go around. To a stiff suspension was mated a Hemi V-8, tuned to deliver 300hp—more than any other American production car in 1955—and it was named for that power. Largely conceived by Chrysler Division chief engineer Bob Rodger, its combination Chrysler/Imperial styling was created by Virgil Exner, who insisted that Rodger's limited-edition high-performance model bear a family resemblance to the standard line. Designated the C-300 (there was never a 300A), what Karl Ludvigsen called the "Beautiful Brute" began production in January 1955. The first, white hardtop was followed by ten red ones, and later Chrysler also built black cars; but white dominated production. It was in some ways a curious combination: a big, luxury, leather-upholstered car with chrome wire wheels, that could run Chrysler's Chelsea, Michigan, proving grounds round the clock for twenty-four hours, touching 140mph.

The 300 was available only as a two-door hardtop, though a Nevada casino asked for a "Chrysler Imperial 300 station wagon," which it duly received: strictly a one-off. The 1956 model, to which the letter "B" was appended on script and badges, continued to use the Imperial grille, New Yorker body and front bumpers, gaining distinction at low cost. A change was the use of painted headlight rims, though a few 300Bs had chrome plated pieces as in 1955. Aside from this, the only significant identifying trait was the swept-up rear fenderline with integral taillights, cleaner than the "Twin Tower" lamps. Under the hood, however, was a 340hp Hemi (350 with 10:1 compression), which made it considerably quicker.

The 1957 300C, with Exner's new styling, was the cleanest of all 300s, with a 375hp version of the new Chrysler 392 V-8. An optional 10:1 compression setup came with a higher-lift cam, delivering between 390 and 400hp. A three-speed TorqueFlite transmission was mated to a 3.36:1 rear axle ratio, and a manual gearbox was standard. Other features attesting to the 300C's performance were new

At the Chelsea Proving Grounds, Chelsea, Michigan: the original 1955 300 poses for the factory photographer. Imperial grille gave the 300 immediate distinction. Most came, as this one, in white with a saddle tan leather interior.

"SilentFlite" fan drive which cut out at 2500rpm to save power, and functional air scoops under the headlamps which channelled air onto the front brake drums. Though not discs, and limited by new 14in wheels, they gave a total lining area of 251 square inches. The front torsion bars were thicker and 40 percent stiffer than New Yorker bars, giving commensurate increases in cornering ability. Power steering was optional but worthwhile, as it required only 3.3 turns lock to lock. *Motor Trend* did 0-60 in eight seconds with the standard model and Torque-Flite, and projected a top speed near the speedometer's maximum of 150mph. Production was up this year and a convertible was introduced for the first time. At Daytona, Red Byron ran the measured mile at 134.108mph. The 300 had dominated stock car racing in 1955-56, and looked to do so again, but

Sophomore year: the 1956-300B offered up to 355hp; leather upholstery with crash-pads were built into the backs of the front seats.

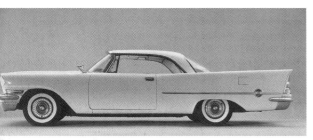

Confident in the lines of the new '57s, Exner placed only a brief strip of bright metal on his new batch of the 300C, the purist development of the "Forward Look." By now the brute was up to 390hp.

The mighty monster at work: a 1957 300C high on the banking and moving fast at the Chrysler Proving Grounds.

in June 1957 the Automobile Manufacturer's Association issued its infamous resolution against performance activities, and the official competition career of the 300 was over.

As a consequence of the racing ban, the addition of optional Bendix Electrojet fuel injection ($400) on the 1958 300D was not widely promoted. The Bendix system added 15hp compared to the carburetor version, at the expense of complexity and difficult maintenance; only sixteen 300Ds were equipped with it. With the standard 380hp engine, *Road & Track* managed 0-60 in 8.4 seconds and a top speed in the neighborhood of 135mph. Dual exhausts, a 300 trademark, were still standard, but curiously the convertible's were smaller than the hardtop's because the reinforced frame got in their way. *Road & Track* thought it would be a better car if the size was cut 25 percent, but nobody paid any attention, even though standard-size car sales were falling off and the imports were advancing strongly.

Nineteen fifty-nine saw a controversial switch to a 413ci wedge-head V-8 and the abandonment of fuel injection. But performance of the 1959 300E topped its predecessor in most tests. Bill Callahan, in *Motor Trend,* confirmed Chrysler Engineering's 0-60 time of 8.3 seconds, against 9.7 for the 300D. Unfortunately, the '59 model was a flop with the public and set a new low for production.

Undaunted, Chrysler launched the unibody 300F for 1960, with a more powerful 413 engine. A fake spare tire outline was added to the deck lid, but enthusiasts yelped loudly and it was dropped for 1961. Optional now was Chrysler Ram Induction manifolding, which gave a large boost in performance, and French Pont-à-Mousson four-speed manual transmission, which should have worked well but was expensive and unpopular. At the most, only fifteen four-speeds were produced. The

The 300D was unchanged, but came with quad headlights as standard. Recession year 1958 held sales to a minimum, creating the rarest 300s to date: only 618 hardtops and 191 convertibles; underhood was the twin four-barrel Hemi with up to 1hp per cubic inch.

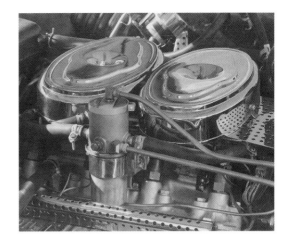

"F" had bucket-like seats and a center console inspired by the X-613 experimental car. Its successor, the 300G, introduced a new heavy-duty three-speed transmission which Chrysler had wanted to have ready for the "F" but was had been instead to rely on the French four-speed. The 300G engine was unchanged, but the cars went back to 15in wheels for better handling and brake cooling. In appearance the "G" was only mildly different from the "F," Chrysler continuing its program of gradual refinements instead of wholesale change.

But 1962 was a year of considerable change. Most obvious, of course, was the new finless styling, and a new, "non-letter-series" 300 introduced to replace the Windsor line. This rode the smaller wheelbase. While ram induction was deleted from the list of standard equipment, the 300G's high performance cam, heavy-duty valve springs, special intake manifold, and mechanical tappets were retained. The result was still pretty impressive: *Speed Mechanics* clocked 0-60 in 6.5 seconds holding the TorqueFlite in "D2" position, and 100mph in less than 16 seconds. Standard equipment included seat belts, leather semi-buckets with console, tachometer, 7.60x15 Goodyear Blue Streak tires, power windows, and the usual 150mph speedometer.

The 1963 300J (the letter "I" was bypassed to avoid confusion) was different in many ways from previous letter series Chryslers. It had an all-new body, like all '63s, but there was no convertible model; it had fifty more horses than the New Yorker, but lacked most of the individuality of letter series models that had gone before. Indeed the 300J looked like any workaday Chrysler until you got up close, and one didn't hear about any performance achievements. It almost seemed as if they were ashamed of it.

For 1959, the 300E exchanged Hemi for wedge-head V-8 but was no less potent; styling, held over with little change, made it distinct from the other '59s; a blacked out grille with four thin bright horizontal bars and 300 badges on the hood quickly distinguish it.

In 1964-65, promotion got moving again on the 300K and 300L. A convertible returned, but the "K," which shared the body design of the 1963 model, had no more horsepower than you could get in the non-letter 300, unless you went for the short ram manifold, dual-barrel carb version, which allowed 30hp more. The successor "L" had 1965's new body styling, but only one engine offering, the New Yorker's optional 360hp unit. Power was down, handling was forgotten, comfort was up; conventionality was the rule.

The 1960 300F shared basic Chrysler body but was again ultra-clean with its short bodyside chrome strip. Swivel seats and a large console housing tachometer, power window controls, two ashtrays, lighters, and center armrests added to the deluxe presentation.

It was also the end of the line. Despite the best two sales years in letter series history, Chrysler Corporation never produced another edition of the "Beautiful Brute." The standard 300s were doing well, and most of the performance interest was in smaller Dodges and Plymouths packing the same kind of big blocks that had powered the letter series.

Identification

1955: Standard Chrysler "Twin-Tower" taillamps combined with Imperial divided egg-crate grille. Small "300" checked-flag badge centered between grilles and on trunk lid. Round parking lamps, single bodyside chrome strip; two-door hardtop the only body style.

1956: Similar to 1955 with rear tailfins housing integrated taillights. "B" added to badges and script.

1957: All-new styling with smooth, tall tailfins housing huge integrated taillights; large, trapezoid egg-crate grille; checked-flag badges replaced by circular, red-white-blue "300C" badge. Convertible model added. For 1957 to 1959, 300 front ends were unique.

1958: "Shrunken" taillights do not appear on the backs of the rear fenders as in 1957. Except for "300D" badges styling was otherwise unchanged.

1959: Front end was similar to 1958, not revised to match other '59 Chryslers: blacked out oblong grille with thin horizontal bars. Red white and blue badge reads "300E." Taillights and rear bumper identical to other '59 models.

1960: Unibody construction. The only letter series with Exner's "toilet seat" spare tire outline on the deck. Blacked out grille with "300F" emblem centrally located by chrome vertical and horizontal bars.

1961: Grille treatment similar to 1960 with red, white, and blue "300G" emblem. Canted quad headlamps, taillamps relocated in horizontal housings under the tailfins, and back-up lamps set into chrome housings at the tops of the fins.

1962: Facelifted extensively at rear with tailfins removed and taillights smoothly integrated into fender tips. Traditional blacked out grille with red, white, and blue "300H" emblem, repeated as usual in the bodyside chrome molding along the doors and rear fenders.

Little change marked the 1961 300G, save for conventional Chrysler restyling, but only 337 of these convertibles were built, making it one of today's most sought-after Letter Series cars. The 300F convertible saw even lower volume.

1963: Restyled in line with other '63 models; convertible model dropped. Blacked out grille remained but red, white, and blue badge was replaced by a black medallion with the model name and letter "J" set in thin white lines. Traditional side molding/emblem combination dropped but the new "J" badge was set into the front fenders.

1964: Similar to 1963 with black badge on grille and fenders now reading THREE HUNDRED K. Convertible model reinstated.

1965: All new styling with concave upper bodysides and full-width area under hood containing horizontal quad headlamps and blacked out grille. Black badge now reading THREE HUNDRED L in grille center lit up when lights were turned on. Painted insert in upper body molding; damascened insert between taillights.

Appraisal

The most sought-after Chryslers of the fifties and early sixties, the letter series 300 through 300H is a thoroughbred of distinguished pedigree, with every right to be revered as the retired champion it is. Through the 300G, it is by comparison to ordinary Chryslers a hard-riding, noisy, rough-idling beast, which returns in exchange body-jolting acceleration and impressive roadability. Though lacking the custom-built quality of previous 300s, the 1962 300H was probably the equal of the 300G in performance, and its thoroughbred characteristics had not entirely been sacrificed to meet the demands of sales and luxury. The 1963-65 300K/J/L are much less distinctive, but still very high performance cars a cut above the norm. Letter series 300s were bid to incredible prices during the "investor" frenzy of the late 1980s; they have gradually subsided, but still cost plenty.

Summary and Prospects

Appreciation on the entire range of letter series Chryslers has been remarkably uniform over the past fifteen years. In 1980 the hardtop-only C300 and 300B led the range, probably because they had been recognized earlier as the very special cars they are. Relatively, these two models have not quite performed with the rest, but 10 percent on your money over the 1980-1995 period can hardly be sneezed at; and meanwhile, look at where the rest of them have been going! Nowhere but up. (I should point out that for consistency, the prices below are all taken in this case from the *Old Cars Value Guide,* which tends to be optimistic; the authoritative CPI guide presently pegs the 1955-56 models at only about $22,000 maximum; later prices are closer together.) Of course, 300C/D/E convertibles were bid up to double these figures at auction six or eight years ago, but their values were

Shorn of tailfins, the 1962 300H was nevertheless unmistakable, with its now-traditional blacked-out, cross-bar grille and clean bodysides punctuated only by a brief chrome strip. With up to 405 hp the "H" was the most powerful 300 yet, but enjoyed one of the shortest production runs, including just 123 of these convertibles.

Specifications
Engines (net hp)
Type: cast-iron V-8, hemi-head (1956-58), wedge-head (1959-65)
331.0ci (3.81 x 3.63), 300hp (1955)
354.0ci (3.91 x 3.63), 340/355hp (1956)
392.0ci (4.00 x 3.90), 375/390hp (1957), 380/390hp (1958)
413.0ci (4.18 x 3.75), 380hp (1959), 375/400hp (1960-61), 380/405hp (1962), 360/390hp (1963-64), 360hp (1965)

Chassis and Drivetrain
Separate chassis frame (1955-59) unit body and frame (1960-61); shaft drive, four-wheel hydraulic brakes, steel wheels. Heavy-duty suspension, heavy-duty torsion bar front suspension (1957-65). PowerFlite automatic transmission (1955), TorqueFlite or three-speed manual transmission (1956-59, 1961), TorqueFlite or four-speed manual transmission (1960); TorqueFlite standard (1962-63); TorqueFlite or four-speed manual transmission (1964-65).

Size and Weight
Wheelbase (in):
126in (1955-62); 122in (1963-64); 124in (1965)
Curb Weight (lb):
1955 4,000lb; 1956 4,150lb; 1957 hardtop 4,235lb, convertible 4,390lb; 1958 hardtop 4,300lb, convertible 4,475lb; 1959 hardtop 4,290lb, convertible 4,350lb; 1960-61 hardtop 4,270lb, convertible 4,310lb; 1962-63 hardtop 4,000lb, convertible 4,080lb; 1964 hardtop 3,965lb, convertible 4,000lb; 1965 hardtop 4,170lb, convertible 4,250lb

Robert M. Rodger, the engineer who deserves most of the credit for the 300's conception, with the massive, ram-induction 390hp V-8 of the 300J. Before he died, a colleague of mine asked Bob if he knew in 1955 that he had created a modern classic. "Yep," he said.

clearly inflated. At today's prices, $60,000 seems a horrendous price for a 300F convertible, and I guess I'd settle for something less than a 95-point show-winner, which will appreciate just as fast if I take care of it.

In terms of appreciation, potential there doesn't seem much to choose from between hardtops and convertibles. But take a look at the production figures: particularly for the 300H hardtop, which is relatively affordable, yet rare. Let's face it, letter series Chryslers cost a bundle; but they are in their way inimitable.

Return on investment (95-point condition 1):

	1980	1995	*Return
1955-56 C300/300B hardtop	$8,000	$36,000	10.6%
1957-59 300C/300E hardtop	$6,500	$43,000	13.5%
1957-59 300C/300E convertible	$8,000	$54,000	13.6%
1960 300F hardtop	$6,700	$52,000	14.7%
1960 300F convertible	$8,000	$66,000	15.2%
1961 300G hardtop	$6,500	$40,000	12.9%
1961-62 300G/300H convertible	$7,500	$52,000	13.9%
1962 300H hardtop	$4,500	$39,000	15.6%
1963-64 300J/300K hardtop	$4,000	$28,000	13.9%
1964 300K convertible	$4,800	$34,000	14.0%
1965 300L hardtop	$3,600	$27,000	14.5%
1965 300L convertible	$4,500	$32,000	14.0%

*compound annual rate of return unadjusted for maintenance, insurance, and running costs

Production

	1955	1956	1957	1958	1959
hardtop, 2dr.	1,725	1,102	1,918	618	550
convertible	0	0	484	191	140

	1960	1961	1962	1963	1964
hardtop, 2dr.	964	1,280	435	400	3,022
convertible	248	337	123	0	625

	1965
hardtop, 2dr.	2,405
convertible	440

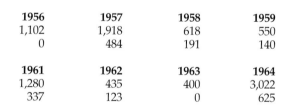

The 300s for 1963-64 looked impressive with Chrysler's newly restyled body and a heavy cross-bar grille. This hardtop was the only model 300J, but a convertible reappeared with 1964's 300K.

Chapter 17

Imperial
1955-61

One can scarcely imagine Cadillac Division quaking in its corporate boots when Chrysler announced that Imperial would be a separate make in 1955. For once, however, Highland Park's timing was perfect: 1955, a banner sales year, marked a vigorous comeback for whole Chrysler line, under the twin impulses of Virgil Exner's styling and traditional fine engineering. From sales of around 5,000 a year, Imperial racked up close to 14,000 in calendar 1955, and not much less in 1956, when most other makes fell off considerably. While a 14,000-unit year was unimpressive by Cadillac standards, it certainly was joyous news at Chrysler, which hadn't built that many Imperials since 1951.

Styling of the '55 and '56 was inspired by Exner's beautiful Parade Phaeton showcars and his first two-seater experimental model, the 1951 Chrysler K-310. Wearing a distinctive grille and elegantly trimmed inside and out, these big sedans and hardtops still look very good today. The '56 gained tailfins and a longer wheelbase—the longest, in fact, of any Imperials short of the seven-passenger cars. The only significant option for 1955-56 was air conditioning ($567); Imperials were equipped as standard with PowerFlite (from 1956 1/2 TorqueFlite) automatic and, surprisingly, won steady laurels in their class in the Mobilgas Economy Runs. The 149.5in wheelbase 1955-56 Crown Imperials replaced all previous Dodge, DeSoto, and Chrysler long-wheelbase cars, but sold in small numbers.

On the strength of its initial acceptance the Imperial blossomed into a three-series line-up for 1957. The two new ranges included the Crown series, which brought back a convertible body style; and the LeBaron, elaborately trimmed four-door sedan and a mid-year four-door hardtop. Restyled with Exner's "Forward Look," the Imperial boasted torsion-bar front suspension, huge tailfins, and a complicated, full-width grille. The formula was successful: Imperial just nipped Lincoln in calendar 1957 production, and would also lead Lincoln in the 1959-60 model years.

Beginning 1957, Crown Imperial limousines were built by Ghia of Turin, who started with unfinished two-door hardtop bodies and added 20.5in

Vintage Exner: the Imperial's bolt egg-crate grille, oversize eagle badge, peaked headlights, and "bombsight" theme of parking and taillights were inspired by Chrysler's new chief stylist, who was strongly influenced by cars of the classic era: late 1920s and early 1930s.

to the wheelbase, reworking the greenhouse and trimming the luxurious interior. Construction of each car took a month and with so much hand work the price was stratospheric: $15,075. Sales were never impressive, but each year brought a new version of the Ghia customs, all of which were impeccably tailored.

The '58 Imperial was changed only slightly—given more horsepower and slightly higher prices—but this too was a case of good timing: 1958 was a recession year and even a complete restyle wouldn't have mattered. Better luck followed in

1959, when sales rose thanks in part to a serious facelift involving a toothy new grille and added side trim. The base Imperial now acquired its own model name, "Custom." Along with other Chrysler products, Imperial switched to the 413ci wedge-head V-8, which provided performance comparable to the Hemi but was more economical to build and maintain. For 1959 through most of the 1960 model year, Imperial's were built in their own plant (ex-Graham-Paige) in Dearborn.

The heroically finned Imperials of the early sixties sold well, though not in record numbers, and the marque's shortlived dominance over Lincoln was

The 1955 Newport coupe with chrome wires seems to look better every year; Exner's well-integrated styling and moderate use of chrome (aft of the grille) were appropriate to the car's $5,000 price and in keeping with Cadillac and Lincoln competition; but their styles were aging while Imperial's was brand new.

The chief change for 1956 was the addition of modest tailfins; rectangular wheel openings were also new. The Imperial name was spelled out in block letters on sides and rear. Right rear fender section swung away to allow access to fuel filler.

eclipsed by the handsome 1961 Lincoln Continentals. Unlike other Chrysler products in 1960, Imperial retained separate body-and-frame construction, which allowed the greater insulation demanded by the need for smooth, silent running. The '60 line was a repeat of '59, with Custom, Crown, and LeBaron ranges, each separated by about $600. Styling was a facelift, but comfort was enhanced with new, high-back driver's seat, adjustable "spot air conditioning," six-way power seat controlled by a single knob, Auto-Pilot cruise control and automatic headlamp dimming. Customs were upholstered in crown-pattern nylon, while Crowns wore nylon/vinyl or leather; wool broadcloth was used for LeBarons.

The 1961 models were altered considerably, though they still used the 1960 shell. Fins were the most blatant ever, and accompanied by a new gimmick: freestanding headlamps, pocketed in the curve of the front fenders, and freestanding taillamps, nestled in the reverse curve of the fins. These, and the infamous dummy spare tire outline often found on Imperial decks, were Classic-era throwbacks introduced by Exner, who admired the designs of the 1930s. Custom, Crown, and LeBaron models were again offered, but the four-door pillar sedans were eliminated.

Identification

1955: Large divided grille composed of thick horizontal and vertical bars with eagle badge centered between; no hood ornament: "Imperial" on small gold plate at leading edge of hood. "Bombsight" taillights. Hardtop known as "Newport" this year only. Round wheel openings.

1956: Similar to 1955 but with prominent tailfins rising from mid-body section and running aft to tips of rear fenders. Both two- and four-door hardtops now known as "Southamptons." Rectangular wheel openings.

1957: All-new styling with full width, ornate grilles; eagle mascot now mounted (as an option) on leading edge of hood; quad or dual headlamps available. Tall tailfins carry a derivation of the previous "bombsight" taillight, with lenses extended aft. Dome-like, wrapover windshield on hardtops and convertibles. Oblong parking lights contained within front bumper. Unusual earmuff-style rear roof quarter (usually painted contrasting color) on hardtops and convertibles. The first American production car with curved side glass.

1958: Styling similar 1957, with three prominent vertical grille dividers; quad headlamps on all models. Round parking lights in front bumper.

1959: Similar to 1957-58, quickly identifiable by bold grillework with five vertical "teeth."

1960: Restyled with open rear quarter windows and abruptly rising tailfins. Fine mesh grille

A new Crown series was added for 1957, containing the first convertible in Imperial's life as a separate make. It sold for over $5,600 and only about 1,200 were built, but it brought new life and prestige to the marque, which was now selling almost as many cars as Lincoln.

contains "Imperial" script; stylized eagle returned to hood. Wide, upwardly flared front bumper with round parking lights underneath.

1961: Sharply pointed tailfins with freestanding "bombsight" taillights hung within a reverse curve on each fin; freestanding classic-style quad headlamps.

Appraisal

Imperials have always brought premium prices compared to Chryslers of the same year, from the time they were new to today's offerings on the muddy fields of Hershey or Carlisle. There seems little difference in value between early four-door sedans and four-door hardtops, but the two-door hardtop, which was worth about 50 percent more than a four-door in 1980, is now worth nearly twice as much. The later four-door hardtops have also come up dramatically in the last fifteen years, the 1957-58 versions scoring the highest rate of appreciation of all the models surveyed below. Convertibles remain the most desirable Imperials, but not by the same margin as they enjoyed in 1980, and rarely has one broken the $30,000 mark to date. Long-wheelbase limousines have moved up nicely, but do note that the long-wheelbase 1955-56 sedan (without division window) is not worth the same as its limo counterpart.

Summary and Prospects

I don't very often recommend investing in a convertible these days, because the prices of most

The 1958 LeBaron sedan looked long but was no larger than the Crown and standard models; what it did offer was a chaste broadcloth monotone interior and more elaborate trim, at a price close to $6,000. These are rare today.

of them have risen to very high levels and I question how much they stand to appreciate compared to hardtops. But the Imperial Crown convertible (1957-61) is undervalued. When you consider that a conventional Cadillac Sixty-two ragtop from the same period now commands $35,000-45,000, the Imperial looks like a bargain. Of course, there are a lot more people interested in Cadillacs than Imperials (just as there were in the fifties). A more depressing comparison might be the 1961 Lincoln Continental four-door convertible, which rarely breaks $20,000 today. Still, I'd take my chances and buy the best Crown convertible I could find. This car is going to move way up in price in the coming decade. Hardtops are equally good invest-

A toothy DeSoto look accompanied the '59 models (the $5774 Crown convertible shown here), which lasted only a year; it was too gaudy even for Virgil Exner, although it outsold the even gaudier Lincoln. Badges on each front fender tip and massive chrome plated bumper added to the heavy look. Ragtops made only 555 sales this year.

ments, especially the two-door versions, and should continue to appreciate sharply in the years ahead. Ghia limos are other-worldly creations, but they need a lot of garage space and aren't much fun to drive.

Return on investment (95-point condition 1):

	1980	1995	*Return
1955-56 4dr. sedan & hardtop	$3,000	$12,000	9.7%
1957-61 sedan, 4dr.	$2,500	$10,000	9.7%
1957-61 hardtop, 4dr.	$2,750	$13,000	11.0%
1955-56 Newport hardtop, 2dr.	$4,500	$22,000	11.2%
1957-58 2dr. hardtops (all)	$3,750	$20,000	11.9%
1955-56 Crown Imperial limousine	$5,500	$20,000	9.0%
1955-56 Crown Imperial sedan	$4,750	$15,000	8.0%
1957-58 Crown convertible	$8,000	$27,500	8.6%
1959-61 Crown convertible	$6,000	$25,000	10.0%
1957-61 Crown Imperial limousine	$6,100	$25,000	9.9%

*compound annual rate of return unadjusted for maintenance, insurance, and running costs

Another successful sales year in 1960 saw a cleaned up Imperial with a fine mesh grille, retaining the towering tailfins, which were now fast becoming passé. Southampton four-door hardtops were now outselling the standard sedans by heavy margins.

Production

	1955	1956			
sedan, 4dr.	7,840	6,821			
hardtop, 4dr.	0	1,543			
hardtop, 2dr.	3,418	2,094			
Crown Imperial limousine	127	175			
Crown Imperial lwb sedan	45	51			

	1957	1958	1959	1960	1961
sedan, 4dr.	5,654	1,926	2,071	2,335	0
hardtop, 4dr.	7,527	1,801	3,984	3,953	4,129
hardtop, 2dr.	4,885	3,336	1,743	1,498	889
Crown sedan, 4dr.	3,642	1,240	1,335	1,594	0
Crown hardtop, 4dr.	7,843	4,146	4,714	4,510	4,769
Crown hardtop, 2dr.	4,199	1,939	1,728	1,504	1,007
Crown convertible	1,167	675	555	618	429
LeBaron sedan, 4dr.	1,729	501	510	592	0
LeBaron hardtop, 4dr.	911	538	522	999	1,026
Crown Imperial limousine	36	31	7	16	9

Specifications
Engines (net hp)
Type: cast-iron V-8, hemi-head (1956-58), wedge-head (1959-61)
331.1ci (3.81 x 3.63in), 250hp (1955), 280hp (1956)
392.0ci (4.00 x 3.90in), 345hp (1957-58), 325hp (1957-59 Crown Imperial)
413.0ci (4.18 x 3.75in), 350hp (1959-61)

Chassis and Drivetrain
Separate chassis frame; shaft drive, four-wheel hydraulic brakes, steel wheels. Automatic transmission standard (PowerFlite 1955-56, TorqueFlite 1956-61).

Size and Weight
Wheelbase (in):
130in (1955), 133in (1956), 129in (1957-61), 149.5in (Crown Imperial)
Curb Weight (lb):
1955-56 4,600lb, Crown Imperial 5,300lb;
1957-61 4,700-4,900lb, Crown Imperial 6,000lb

Exner's baroque designs reached their height (or bottom, depending on your viewpoint) on the 1961 Imperial, which had more abrupt but yet taller shark-fin rear fenders and freestanding headlamps and taillamps as Virgil tried another classic era look. At only 429, the '61 had the lowest production of any convertible in this chapter.

★★★

Chapter 18

Crown Imperial
1955-65

In 1955, Chrysler's "professional car" business (limousines and executive cars) was riding entirely on the Crown Imperial, which emerged as the corporation's only long-wheelbase model, following the demise of those body styles on the chassis of junior makes after 1954. On paper the Crown had much going for it: new status as a separate make a cut above Chrysler, Virgil Exner's fine new styling, and a Hemi V-8 with more horsepower than ever before. But the results could only be viewed as disappointing. Volume failed to top 200 '55s, and the following year they made only 226. Early in 1955, management made the decision that such small sales didn't justify the factory space at Detroit.

Thus, for 1957, they dropped all pretense of a rival to the dominant Cadillac Seventy-five in favor of an upmarket approach: the Ghia Crown Imperial. This was a sensible way to preserve at least the suggestion of a professional car business, since Ghia was able to tool the new Crown Imperial, pro-

vided Chrysler shipped the basic "kit" to the Ghia works at Turin, Italy.

Each Ghia Crown Imperial began as an unfinished two-door hardtop body mounted on a rigid convertible chassis, shipped to Italy with all parts intact. Ghia cut the cars apart, added 20 1/2in to the wheelbase, reworked the greenhouse, fitted and trimmed a luxurious interior, and finished the body with 150lb of lead filler. Construction of each car took a month; initial delays made the '57 a very late introduction, priced at a stratospheric $15,075. (Since Ghia's bill per car was an alleged $15,000, Chrysler clearly was building Crown Imperials for prestige, not profits.)

After building a mere seven Crown Imperials in 1959, sixteen in 1960, and nine in 1961, production stopped for 1962, then resumed a year later, but with hardly greater numbers. Only 132 Ghia Crown Imperials had been built by the time the line ended in 1965, but all of them were impressive cars, beautifully tailored. Air conditioning and

Very refined indeed were the 1955-56 Detroit-built Crown Imperials, priced at just over $7,000 on a stretched 149.5in wheelbase. The limousine (shown) had a division window; only about 170 were built, most of them limousines, and they are extremely scarce today.

Tailfins were welded on with ungainly brightwork to cover the seam on 1956 Crown Imperials. Because of the fender rework, the body molding had to end short of the rear fender, where five hashmarks were applied; this was not as successful as the '55 workout, although sales were up.

An early Crown Imperial limousine, one of only thirty-six '57 models, outside the Ghia works in Torino, Italy. Farming out the semi-custom job to Ghia seemed like a good idea, but resulted in very low production.

A special Crown Imperial with a transparent rear roof quarter, specially built for the visit of Queen Elizabeth II to Canada in 1959. Where is this car today? Has it survived?

Two approaches to the Ghia roofline for 1960, with closed and open quarter lights. Exner's earmuff roof styling was conducive to styling tricks like this which met varying customer tastes.

A '61 Ghia Crown in Manhattan, one of only nine built that year, all limousines. In 1962 production was temporarily phased out.

One of the thirteen 1963 limousines, with Exner's classic-inspired freestanding headlamps. Still riding the original 149.5in wheelbase, the '63 was a car of tremendous presence.

power-everything were standard, and at least from 1960 there were three separate heaters. While each successive model reflected the styling features of its model year, there was little change under the skin. The final run of only ten 1965 models came on the same, 149 1/2in wheelbase as the 1955 models, and after ten years of production the price had risen only modestly, to $18,000.

Commencing in the late 1960s, long-wheelbase Imperials were built by specialty body manufacturers, notable among these being the Stageway Company, which offered limousines on a staggering 163in wheelbase in 1969-70. But these were built in very tiny quantities, and Chrysler's participation in the "professional car" business tapered off to nothing in the 1970s. It took Lee Iacocca to revive the concept with LeBaron mini-limousines based on the "K car" platform in the early 1980s.

Identification

1955-56: Styling the same as conventional models, (split egg-crate grille with large eagle badge centered, "bombsight" taillamps), but with a longer wheelbase. Truncated tailfins on 1956 models. Round wheel openings both years.

1957: All-new styling with full width, ornate grille; eagle mascot now mounted on leading edge of hood; quad or dual headlamps available. Tall tailfins carry a derivation of the previous "bombsight" taillight, with lenses extended aft. Oblong parking lights contained within front bumper.

Fine mesh grille exclusive to Crown Imperial. "Gull-wing" bumpers were one year only.

1958: Styling similar 1957, horizontal bar grille with three prominent vertical divides; quad headlamps on all models. Round parking lights in front bumper. Conventional bumpers.

1959: Similar to 1957-58, quickly identifiable by bold grillework with five vertical "teeth" and "IMPERIAL" name on hood spelled in block letters rather than script; eagle device eliminated from hood. LeBarons carried name in script on front fenders.

1960: Major facelift with fine mesh grille containing "Imperial" script; stylized eagle returned to hood at the head of a center chrome strip. Wide, upwardly flared front bumper with round parking lights underneath.

1961: Sharply pointed tailfins with freestanding "bombsight" taillights hung within a reverse curve on each fin; freestanding classic-style quad headlamps flank a fine mesh horizontal bar grille with stylized eagle emblem ranged right.

1962: No Crown Imperials were produced.

1963: Freestanding quad headlamps flanked a grille composed of stacked oblong sections, divided by a vertical rectangle containing an eagle emblem. Taillamps were carried in the slim trailing edges of the rear fenders. A stand-up hood ornament appeared for the first time on a Crown Imperial.

1964: A restyle saw the disappearance of freestanding headlamps; quad headlamps were now carried in extremities of a divided, horizontal bar grille and the fenderline was edged in chrome, similar to the concurrent Lincoln Continentals. Simulated spare tire "bulge" in rear deck and bumper.

Elwood Engel's styling ideas favored a crisper look, but the Exner roof flavor was retained on Ghia Crowns for 1964-65. In this factory photo, the car is wearing a "LeBaron" nameplate merged with a Ghia badge and a Chrysler pentastar: the full assortment!

1965: Mesh grille divided into four sections; headlamps covered by glass panels. Rear end treatment unchanged.

Appraisal

The same appraisal applies to these as to earlier long-wheelbase professional Chryslers, although the Ghia Crown Imperial is a true throwback to the semi-custom body era, built with great care and attention to detail, commensurately rare and not often found in superb condition. Whether they're going anywhere on the collector car market is debatable. Though the 1955-56 limousines have risen in value faster than the long wheelbase sedans, the 1957 and later Ghias (produced as limos only) have not performed as well as their extreme scarcity and semi-custom nature would suggest. There is a limited buyer group for this sort of car, storage being a major consideration. Still, they're a wonderful, otherworldly sight on the road, and a far cry from the rather tamely styled limousines of the present day.

Summary and Prospects

The 1955-56 Chrysler-built Crown Imperials were extremely solid long-wheelbase models which still look impressive today. Limousine design has not changed so much, after all, over the years. Ghia-built Crown Imperials relied on 150lb of body filler, which created rust problems as time went on. Survivors are not common, and many of those still alive are subject in various degrees to rust and corrosion. This consideration is paramount in selecting any Crown Imperial today. The costliness of Hemi engine parts is also a consideration on cars built through 1958.

Return on investment (95-point condition 1):

	1980	1995	*Return
1955-56 long wb sedans	$4,500	$14,000	7.9%
1955-56 limousines	$5,000	$20,000	9.7%
1957-65 Ghia limousine	$6,000	$25,000	10.0%

*compound annual rate of return unadjusted for maintenance, insurance, and running costs

Production

	1955	1956	1957	1958	1959
long w.b. sedan, 8 pass.	45	51	0	0	0
limousine	127	175	36	31	7

	1960	1961	1963	1964	1965
limousine	16	9	13	10	10

(No production in 1962)

After the end of the Ghia Crowns in 1965, specialty manufacturers built a small number of long-wheelbase Imperials. Shown are the 1967 LeBaron limousine by Stageway and the 1972 (with 1973 grille) government limousine by Hess & Eisenhardt.

Specifications
Engines (net hp)
Type: cast-iron V-8, hemi-head (1956-58), wedge-head (1959-65)
331.1ci (3.81 x 3.63in), 250hp (1955), 280hp (1956)
392.0ci (4.00 x 3.90in), 325hp (1959), 350hp (1960)
413.0ci (4.18 x 3.75in), 350hp (1961), 340hp (1963-65)

Chassis and Drivetrain
Separate chassis frame, shaft drive, four-wheel hydraulic brakes, steel wheels. Automatic transmission standard (PowerFlite 1955-56, TorqueFlite 1956-65).

Size and Weight
Wheelbase (in): 149.5in
Curb Weight (lb):
1955-56 long w.b. sedans 5,200lb, limousines 5,300lb;
1957-61 Ghia limousines 6,000lb; 1963-65 Ghia limousines 6,100lb

★★

Chapter 19

Newport & 300
1962-71

Chrysler's response to the compact car boom of the early sixties was to declare, "There will never be a small Chrysler." To underline this determination, the division brought out a more competitive line of big Chryslers. In 1961, while rivals like Buick, Olds, Pontiac, and Mercury were all fielding compacts, Chrysler introduced the under-$3,000 Newport, priced hundreds below the Windsor, a model so popular that it replaced the Windsor entirely by 1962. That same year, Chrysler offered a big-car alternative to the sporty compacts like the Buick Skylark and Olds F-85: the "non-letter" 300, flashily trimmed in the style of the letter series, sold mainly in sporty body styles and slotted neatly in a market niche halfway between the Newport and New Yorker. The 300 lasted through 1971. While no muscle car, it always had a few more cubic inches or horsepower than the Newport. Bucket seats, center console, and sporty, color-keyed interiors combined with '62s new finless styling to create a popular new addition to the Chrysler line-up.

Virgil Exner left Chrysler after shaping the restyled 1963-64 models, chunky looking cars with a wide, inverted trapezoid grille, horizontally paired headlamps, and no tailfins. Ads said these Chryslers had "the crisp, clean custom look." They were hefty and purposeful looking, but the advent of new talent at Chrysler Styling meant they wouldn't be around more than two years.

Their 1965 replacement arrived three years after Exner's replacement as chief of design: Elwood Engel, the former Ford designer generally credited with the elegant 1961 Lincoln Continental. Engel favored smooth, concave-sided bodies with fender tops edged in bright metal, a shape which continued more or less through 1968. For 1969, Engel came up with more rounded, less bulky "fuselage styling." Engel Chryslers were shorter than their predecessors, but their wheelbase was 124in, up 2in from 1964. This added significant passenger space while deleting a considerable amount of overhang.

In 1967 the Newport was joined by the Newport Custom, priced about $200 higher. Promoted as "a giant step in luxury, a tiny step in price," the

A new styling era was proclaimed by the de-finned 1962s, though the change was evolutionary since stylists retained the 1961 front end. Handsome "non-letter" 300 with bucket seats and traditional 300 styling was quite popular.

Custom comprised two-door and four-door hardtops and a four-door sedan. Deluxe interiors were finished in jacquard or textured vinyl upholstery and seats had pull-down center armrests. The dashboard of a fully equipped Newport Custom had eight toggle switches, three thumbwheels, sixteen pushbuttons, three sliding levers, and twelve other controls which, Chrysler proclaimed, "put you in charge of almost every option in the book." They certainly gave you enough to do with your fingers.

After the luxurious New Yorker Town & Country wagon was dropped following 1965, Newport wagons were the only ones in the Chrysler line. All-vinyl upholstery was used, instead of the cloth/vinyl combination of other Newports. Standard features included power steering, power brakes, and automatic transmission. Wagons also had a three-in-one front seat that looked like a conventional bench; each half could be adjusted individually, and there was a reclining seatback on the passenger's side. For 1969-70, the Town & Country was a separate model in its own right.

Town & Country Newport, 1962, handily outsold the larger New Yorker with a price around $3,500. There is a small collector craze for hardtop wagons, and this is one of the most attractive years for the Chryslers.

The "crisp, clean, custom look" (and the last of Exner's influence) is displayed by a 1963 "non letter" 300 convertible. In this kind of perfect condition it could bring close to $15,000 today, but more worn examples cost half as much. The "Pace Setter" trim package is worth perhaps 10 percent more.

A 1964 Newport hardtop wagon; styling changes this year were chiefly to the grillework.

Chrysler enjoyed record calendar year production in 1968, and did almost as well in 1969. The '69s were handsome, with a combination bumper/grille and clean, smooth contours. If not the most beautiful Chryslers of the decade (I think that prize should go to the '62s) they were pretty close. Wheelbases remained at 124in but the cars were longer, almost 225in overall, and 80in wide—about as big as the American passenger car would get.

On into the seventies, there was no "small Chrysler"—until 1975. That was the year the Cordoba was announced.

Identification

1962: Similar to the '61 up front, but shorn of tailfins, with the taillights inserted flush in the upper trailing ends of the rear fenders. 300s had a blacked-out grille with a central, red white, and blue badge located by vertical and horizontal brightmetal bars. Headlamps on all models were vertically slanted.

1963: Complete restyle with slab sides, small round taillights, horizontal headlamps, and minimal chrome trim. The 300s continued to use the distinctive blacked-out grille. 300 Pace Setter convertible and two-door hardtop had checkered flag emblems on front fenders and a squarish (instead of round) steering wheel.

1964. A facelift model easily identified by grillework: on the Newport, an emblem centered on each of three cross-bars; on the 300, a blacked out grille cavity with much heavier crossbars and anodized silver trim. Small tailfins.

1965: Completely restyled with a broader, flatter grille and extruded side molding outlined with stainless steel at the top beltline. Headlamps set within the grille area. Horizontal taillights set within anodized panel under deck lid. 300 continued with a blacked-out grille and star-shaped emblem, and had glass-covered headlamps.

1966: Mild facelift with painted insert on lower trim moldings and nameplates on rear quarter panels. 300 dropped the glass-covered headlamps and cross-bar grille and adopted a more conventional grille with a thick horizontal bar; 300s also had dummy extractor vents on lower front fenders.

1967: Extensive facelift introduced a new two-door hardtop roofline with a closed-in rear quarter resembling that of a convertible. Standard Newport was plainly trimmed; lower sill molding was its only side trim. Newport Custom had more side trim, skirted rear fenders, and an upgraded interior with center armrests. 300 rear end was unique to that model: taillamps sloped from deck to bumper height, back-up lamps were set into the bumper; crossbar style grille and spinner hubcaps also distinguished the 300.

1968: Another facelift gave a much squarer look. Vee'd mesh type grille with vertical Chrysler badge on Newport. Newport Customs carried identifying script on front fenders, Newports on the rear. 300s had blacked out grille with hidden headlamps and full-width horizontal double bar; also chrome hashmarks on lower front fenders and 300 badges.

1969: All-new "Fuselage" styling with combination bumper-grille and smooth, curved sides. Newport grilles composed of fine horizontal blades. Again, Newports carried identifying script on rear fender, Newport Customs on front; Customs also had a rear deck "beauty panel" with vertically segmented grille pattern running across taillights. Wagons were separately grouped as a Town & Country model this year. 300s were styled similarly to Newports, with the model name spelled out in block letters on rear quarter panels; grille was blacked out with cross bars and headlamps were hidden as in 1968.

1970: The 300 again had hidden headlamps, a 300 emblem centered on a blacked-out grille flanked by horizontal moldings which did not join in the middle. Newport and Newport Custom are again identifiable by script placed on rear fenders (Newport) or front fenders (Newport Custom). Both carried a new grille made of closely spaced vertical blades in three horizontal tiers, along with a concave taillight panel with oblong, chrome-banded taillights.

1971: Facelift with a new grille composed of two thin horizontal bars against a black background. Newport Royal was a new, lower-priced Newport with a smaller, 360ci engine, and a truncated body side molding that ended just forward of the front door. Newport carried full body side moldings, Newport Custom had an upgraded interior with folding center armrests. All Newports were identified by script. The 300, in its last year, continued with its distinctive grille and hidden headlamps; '71s also featured color-coordinated vinyl side rub strips and special hubcaps.

Special Models

1963: 300 Pace Setter two-door hardtop and convertible, commemorated Chrysler's selection as

A new grille and roofline marked the 1966s, and "non-letter" 300s like this hardtop can be quickly distinguished by dummy vents on the lower front fenders; the stand-up hood ornament bears "300" numerals

All-new, and one of the best looking Chryslers of the decade, the '65 was styled by Elwood Engel along lines he'd developed on the Lincoln Continentals (note crisp bodyside molding and square ends). In prime condition, this Newport convertible can be bought for under five figures, but the 300s (letter series and "non-letter") cost considerably more.

The 1967 Newport Custom hardtop and "non-letter" 300 convertible. The Custom was a new line of up-market Newports; two-door hardtop styling with reverse slanted rear side windows was also new this year. Today the Newport hardtops are "all through" at $6,500, but the 300 convertible in top condition can bring more than twice that.

pace car for the 1963 Indianapolis 500. They are identified by crossed checkered-flag emblems and special trim.

1964: Special 300 for the spring selling season: silver exterior, black vinyl roof, black leather and vinyl interior, star-shaped 300 insignia at C-pillar on hardtops and on front fender of convertibles.

1968: models, look for the "Sportsgrain" option (simulated wood paneling), a $126 extra on Newport hardtops and convertibles which recalls the old Town & Country convertibles of the late forties. Newport Special two- and four-door hardtops were also available with turquoise color schemes, later extended to the 300 series. Sportsgrain production: 965 two-door hardtops, only 175 convertibles.

1970: High performance 300H featured 440 engine with Hurst shifter, heavy duty suspension, styled road wheels, and raised white leather tires. All 300Hs had saddle leather bucket seats, a fiberglass power bulge with functional air scoop, rotary hood latches, a fiberglass deck with integral spoiler; they were painted white with satin tan color accents. Production was only 400 units.

1970: A special order Cordoba hardtop (two or four doors) was offered on the Newport, with gold paint and matching vinyl covered top, "Aztec eagle"

Chrysler is nothing if not devoted to tradition. Today it's the original radiator badge; in 1968 it was the Town & Country, sort of, making a reappearance as something besides a station wagon. Fake wood

"Sportsgrain" finish was ordered on 965 coupes and only 175 convertibles. It easily adds $1,000 to the price of either one on today's market.

embossed vinyl interior, special badging, ventless side windows on two-door models, special wheel-covers and trip odometer. Production was 1,873 four-door hardtops and 1,838 two-door hardtops.

Also seen this year was the "Newport 440," powered by the 440 New Yorker V-8 and equipped with vinyl body side moldings, vinyl covered roof, standard TorqueFlite, and aluminized mufflers and tailpipes.

Appraisal

These are big, heavy cars with a thirst for high octane fuel, which may incur driveability problems under modern conditions. Another consideration as we get into later model Chryslers is the inability of their air conditioning systems to adapt to the new federally-mandated Freon, which will rot out the rubber fittings on pre-1993 systems: as overt an attempt to encourage disuse of old cars as any the Feds have come up with yet.

Summary and Prospects

The special models listed above are the cars to look for; after that, stick with the 300 series for maximum investment value. Among Newports, the best buys are, as always, the convertible models, which are still available at modest prices. (Convertibles were built in both Newport and 300 lines until 1971, when they were all dropped.) There is little indication of major gains in value for these cars, but clean ones ought to keep pace with inflation. The 300H is the most collectible model in this chapter, though not necessarily the best investment: note its relatively slower value appreciation below. The fact that it is a hardtop is a determining point: had there been a convertible, it would be worth over $30,000 today.

If you like enormous cars, the 1970 Chrysler 300 is worth considering, especially if you find one that looks like this. It's hard to criticize its styling, though assembly quality was mediocre, and with the 440 V-8 still standard, it could run with the best of the '70 field.

The most collectible Chrysler in this chapter: the 1970 300-H (for "Hurst") hardtop packs road wheels, H70x15 white-letter tires, 440 engine, heavy duty suspension, gold and white paint job, matte black hood with scoop and hold-down locks, rear deck spoiler, special grille color, and Hurst floor shifter for its automatic gearbox. Four hundred were built and there are still some around to find. The best ones are worth over $10,000, about the same as a standard 300 convertible.

The 1969 "non-letter" 300 hardtop cost $4,000 new, and the best examples today are just exceeding that value. This factory photo is meant to connote sportiness, but severe body roll is evident, and this one is not moving at really high speed.

Specifications

Engines (net hp)
Type: cast-iron V-8
360ci (4.00 x 3.58in), 255hp (1971 Newport)
361ci (4.12 x 3.38in), 265hp (1962-64 Newport)
383ci (4.25 x 3.38in), 270hp (1965-67 Newport, optional 1965 300),
375hp (1971 Newport Custom & wagons, optional 1971 Royal), 290hp (1968-70 Newport)
383ci (4.25 x 3.38in), 300hp (optional 1971 Newport), 305hp (1962-64 300), 315hp (1965-66 300, optional 1965 Newport), 325hp (optional 1966-67 Newport), 330hp (optional 1968-70 Newport)
413ci (4.18 x 3.75in), 340/360hp (optional 1964 300); 360hp (optional 1965 300)
440ci (4.32 x 3.75in), 350hp (1967-70 300, optional 1967, 1969-70 wagons), 375hp (optional all 1968-70 except wagons)
440ci (4.32 x 3.75in), 370hp (optional all 1971 models)

Chassis and Drivetrain
Unit body and frame; shaft drive, four-wheel hydraulic brakes, steel wheels. TorqueFlite automatic transmission optional.

Size and Weight
Wheelbase (in):
122in (1962-64); 124in, wagons 121in (1965-66); 124in, wagons 122in (1967-71)
Curb Weight (lb):
3,700-4,200lb; wagons 4,200-4,500lb

Return on investment (95-point condition 1):

	1980	1995	*Return
1962-71 sedans & 4dr hardtops	$2,000	$5,000	6.3%
1962-71 Town & Country wagons	$2,200	$4,500	4.9%
1962-65 Newport convertible	$2,700	$10,000	9.2%
1962-64 300 convertible	$4,500	$14,000	7.9%
1963 300 Pace Setter 2dr hardtop	$3,350	$8,000	6.0%
1963 300 Pace Setter convertible	$4,000	$15,000	9.3%
1965-67 300 convertible	$4,000	$15,000	9.3%
1965-66 Newport convertible	$3,500	$9,500	6.9%
1967-70 Newport convertible	$2,500	$9,000	9.0%
1968-70 300 convertible	$3,100	$13,500	10.4%
1970 300-H 2dr hardtop	$3,500	$12,500	8.9%

*compound annual rate of return unadjusted for maintenance, insurance, and running costs

First appearance of the name "Cordoba" in Chrysler's lexicon was a trim option for 1970: not highly collectible, but interesting historically.

Production

	1962	1963	1964	1965	1966
Newport:					
hardtop, 2dr.	11,910	9,809	10,579	23,655	37,622
sedan, 4dr.	54,813	49,067	55,957	61,054	74,964
sedan, 4dr. 6 window	0	0	0	12,411	9,432
hardtop, 4dr.	8,712	8,437	9,710	17,0622	4,966
convertible	2,051	2,093	2,176	3,192	3,085
Town & Country, 6passenger	3,271	3,618	3,720	4,683	9,035
Town & Country, 9passenger	2,363	2,948	3,041	3,738	8,567
300:					
hardtop, 2dr.	11,341	9,423	18,379	11,621	24,103
sedan, 4dr.	1,801	1,625	2,078	0	2,353
sedan, 4dr., 6 window	0	0	0	2,187	0
hardtop, 4dr.	10,030	9,915	11,460	12,452	20,642
convertible	1,848	1,535	1,401	1,418	2,500
Pace Setter hardtop, 2dr.	0	306	0	0	0
Pace Setter convertible	0	1,861	0	0	0

	1967	1968	1969	1970	1971
Newport (Town & Country a separate model in 1969-70)					
hardtop, 2dr.	26,583	36,768	33,639	21,664	13,549
Royal hardtop, 2dr.	0	0	0	0	8,500
sedan, 4dr.	48,945	61,436	55,083	39,285	24,834
Royal sedan, 4dr.	0	0	0	0	19,662
hardtop, 4dr.	14,247	20,191	20,608	16,940	10,800
Royal hardtop, 4dr.	0	0	0	0	5,188
convertible	2,891	2,847	2,169	1,124	0
Town & Country, 6passenger	7,183	9,908	10,108	5,686	5,697
Town & Country, 9passenger	7,520	12,223	14,408	9,583	10,993
Newport Custom:					
hardtop, 2dr.	14,193	10,341	10,995	6,639	5,527
sedan, 4dr.	23,101	16,9151	8,401	13,767	11,254
hardtop, 4dr.	12,728	11,640	15,981	10,873	10,207
300:					
hardtop, 2dr.	11,556	16,953	16,075	9,684	7,256
300H hardtop, 2dr.	0	0	0	400	0
hardtop, 4dr.	8,744	15,507	14,464	9,846	6,683
convertible	1,594	2,161	1,933	1,077	0

★★

Chapter 20

New Yorker
1962-71

For the New Yorker and Chrysler, the sixties started slow, picked up in the middle, and tailed off toward the end. Vast changes were evident in the corporation by 1969. Quality control, neglected for years, became an end in itself as engineers struggled to correct Chrysler's reputation for poor body durability since the '57 models. The old centralized corporation had been decentralized under President Tex Colbert; his successor, Lynn Townsend, recentralized it, but retained divisional identity and traditional nomenclature like the New Yorker.

Like all other Chryslers in 1962, the New Yorker lost its tailfins and gained one of the nicest looking bodies of the decade. Traditionally up-market, it rode a 126in wheelbase, 4in longer than all other Chryslers, but the following year the shorter wheelbase was adopted across the boards. This did not hamper New Yorker sales, which were strong in the mid-sixties. Special edition Chryslers usually appeared on the junior models, but in 1963 there

was a unique mid-year New Yorker, the "Salon," a special four-door hardtop with air conditioning, AM/FM radio, auto-pilot, power brakes/steering/seats/ windows all standard, plus color-keyed wheel covers and vinyl padded top.

Throughout the period under discussion, New Yorkers were powered by V-8s in excess of 400ci; they were thirsty, big, and luxurious. Again with the new generation Engel styling of 1965 the New Yorker followed suit, gaining a few inches, but the ultra-posh New Yorker Town & Country was dropped after this year. In 1969 the New Yorker version of "fuselage styling" was an especially handsome workout.

Model year 1971 was the last for "fuselage styling," though the 1972-73 models continued to be based on the 1969 shell. Styling remained clean overall, even if easy-switch items like grilles, taillights, and side decoration became a bit more tacky with time.

Identification

All models are clearly identifiable by New Yorker script.

1962: Similar to 1961 up front, but without tailfins. Ten vertical hashmarks on sides of rear fenders.

1963: Complete restyle with slab sides, small round taillights, horizontal headlamps, and minimal chrome trim. Six vertical hashmarks mounted low on front fenders under New Yorker nameplate. Top series was the Salon four-door hardtop.

1964. A facelift identified by fine mesh grillework: New Yorker Salon series continued to offer standard luxury accessories at the highest prices. Two-door hardtop model added.

1965: Completely restyled with extruded, curving sides, upper bodyside molding finished in bright metal. Glass covered headlamps flanking a bold grille with prominent vertical and horizontal cross-hatching. Sedan was the six-window type.

1966: Mild facelift New Yorker medallions behind wheelhouse on lower front fenders; last year for six-window sedan body.

1967: Extensive facelift introduced a new two-door hardtop roofline with a closed-in rear quarter resembling that of a convertible. New Yorker

Built for the last time on a 126in wheelbase, the 1962 New Yorker achieved its usual 20,000 sales. Pillarless styling looked especially nice this model year; the four-door hardtop is worth up to $6,000 in prime condition today, the two-door hardtop $1,000 more.

taillights wrap around at the sides and rear wheel openings are skirted.

1968: Another facelift with a pointed grille composed of fine mesh separated by a broad horizontal bar; square headlight bezels were unique to the New Yorker.

1969: All-new "Fuselage" styling with smooth, curving body sides. Special New Yorker grille composed of prominent horizontal bars over blacked out grille sections; bright metal trim on lower body parts, headlights spaced wider than on junior models.

1970: Facelift; grille featured prominent horizontal and vertical bars; broad trim on lower body fore to aft; horizontal format taillights.

1971: Facelift with a more elaborate grille than junior models and more standard luxury items, including fully carpeted trunk, Cairo cloth, and vinyl upholstery, skirted rear fenders.

Appraisal

While considerably more luxurious than the 300 and Newport, the New Yorker does not command more collector loyalty; indeed, the lack of a convertible model starting in 1962 means that there is no outstandingly valuable or highly collectible model. But certain models are more equal than others. Particularly desirable is the luxurious, limited edition 1963-64 Salon, which saw only a shade more than 2,200 copies during its two years of production.

The real sleeper, overlooked by many, is the 1964 two-door hardtop, the most luxurious pillarless coupe Chrysler built that year. Missing from many listings, this is the rarest individual model New Yorker ever built, with a production run of only 300 units.

Driveability is a problem with these cars, since they mostly require high octane fuel and are overpowered and underbraked. Quality control was not as good as it should have been in a car of this class. From a design standpoint, however, some models

With a shared wheelbase with the Newport for 1963, the Town & Country wagon was less massive, but no less expensive at close to $5,000. Price guides and asking prices show a 40 percent bulge in what collectors pay for New Yorkers over Newports, despite their equal size.

were very good. Most collectors tend to prefer earlier models, particularly the '62 and '65, which are most desirable from an aesthetic standpoint. Chrysler styling was very good in both these years, better than the subsequent facelifts. A smaller school prefers the chunky 1963-64 body style, the last hurrah of Virgil Exner.

Summary and Prospects

Roughly speaking, after you deduct for maintenance, insurance, and running costs, these New Yorkers have appreciated about at the rate of inflation, which means that if you invested 5,000 1995 dollars in over fifteen years and want to sell it, you'll probably realize about 5,000 1995 dollars.

The limited edition New Yorker Salon for 1963 and 1964, equipped with air conditioning, AM/FM radio, auto-pilot, power brakes/steering/seats/ windows all

standard, plus color-keyed wheel covers and vinyl padded top: these are definitely New Yorkers to look for.

Stylists succeeded in making the all-new 1965 New Yorker more important looking than the Newport and 300, with full-length lower bodyside trim that emphasized its low lines, a busier grille, vinyl covered "C" pillars, and glass-covered headlamps. A car in prime condition should not cost you more than $5,000, but they are hard to find.

Some New Yorkers have done better than others. In 1980, virtually all "condition 1" cars were worth about two grand; today, there's a $3,500 spread. Of course in 1980, the youngest were less than a decade old, and still depreciating. Since then, collectors have sorted out the wheat from the chaff.

A very collectible model from this period is the 1963-64 Salon four-door hardtop. The New Yorker Town & Country, possibly the most luxurious station wagon Detroit ever built, has also done reasonably well; its low production and disappearance after 1965 are two chief reasons for its gains in value. Finally, there's a definite tailing off in value after the 1968 model year. This is most likely due to the less individual styling of the 1969-71 cars and to their driveability problems. They were the first Chryslers seriously effected by Federal air pollution and safety regulations, and the company's solutions to Federal mandates in these years were not always elegant. Engines don't run as well, performance suffers, and the glitzy New Yorker image doesn't take well to expanses of flat black vinyl and "safety" dashboards.

Production

	1962	1963	1964	1965	1966
sedan, 4dr.	12,056	14,884	15,443	16,239	13,025
hardtop, 4dr.	6,646	10,229	10,887	21,110	26,599
Salon hardtop, 4dr.	0	593	1,621	0	0
hardtop, 2dr.	0	0	*300	9,357	7,955
Town & Country wagon, 6pass.	738	3,618	1,190	1,368	0
Town & Country wagon, 9pass.	793	2,948	1,603	1,697	0

	1967	1968	1969	1970	1971
sedan, 4dr.	10,907	13,092	12,253	9,389	9,850
hardtop, 4dr.	21,665	26,991	27,157	19,903	20,633
hardtop, 2dr.	6,885	8,060	7,539	4,917	4,485

*questionable

Return on investment (95-point condition 1):

	1980	1995	*Return
1962 four-door sedan	$1,900	$5,000	6.7%
1962 four-door hardtop	$2,100	$6,500	7.9%
1963-64 Salon four-door hardtop	$1,800	$7,000	9.5%
1962-65 Town & Country wagons	$1,800	$6,500	9.0%
1964 two-door hardtop	$1,900	$8,500	10.6%
1965-68 two-door hardtop	$2,100	$7,500	8.9%
1969-71 two-door hardtop	$2,000	$5,000	6.3%
1965-68 four-door models	$2,000	$6,000	7.6%
1969-71 four-door models	$1,800	$5,000	7.1%

*compound annual rate of return unadjusted for maintenance, insurance, and running costs

Specifications
Engines (net hp)
Type: cast-iron V-8.
413.0ci (4.18 x 3.75in), 340hp (1962-65),
440.0ci (4.32 x 3.75in), 350hp (1966-70), 335hp (1971)
440.0ci (4.32 x 3.75in), 375hp (optional 1967-70), 370hp (1971)

Chassis and Drivetrain
Unit body and frame; shaft drive, four-wheel hydraulic brakes, steel wheels. TorqueFlite automatic transmission standard.

Size and Weight
Wheelbase (in):
126in (1962), 122in (1963-64), 121in (1965 wagons), 124in (1965-71)
Curb Weight (lb):
1962-64 4,000lb, Salon 4,250lb; Town & Country wagons 4,250lb, 4,650lb in 1965; 1965-71 about 4,300lb

The smooth "fuselage styled" 1971 New Yorker with optional electric sliding sunroof, a desirable feature. There is less to distinguish this New Yorker from the Newport than on earlier models, though price guides, if not asking prices, suggest it's worth about 20 percent more, car for car.

Striking new formal roof quarters and slant-back rear side windows marked all 1968 hardtops; New Yorker received a rear grille, another touch borrowed from Lincoln's Continental, with taillights neatly built in at the outside. Note also rear marker lights.

Chapter 21

Imperial
1962-68

The sixties were the make-or-break decade for Imperial as a separate, top-of-the-line make distinct from Chrysler, and by 1970 the concept was broken. The broad Imperial line of models, which had existed since the separate make was declared in 1955, tapered off rapidly in the sixties. For its last seven years Imperial struggled on in limited numbers, a luxury clone of Chrysler. Then it was summarily dropped, although it would appear later as a "personal luxury" coupe to compete with the Thunderbird and Continental Marks (in which guise it did no better).

For the first few years after 1955, Imperial had looked like a real contender, and in a couple of model years (1959-60) it had actually outsold Lincoln. But the crisp 1961 Lincoln Continental put paid to Imperial once and for all, enjoying unprecedented popularity while the Chrysler luxury make achieved only a fraction of Lincoln sales from 1961 onward.

An archetypal Imperial, the 1962 LeBaron Southampton, with freestanding headlamps and the remains of tailfins. Quirky taillights are an ornate excess, but they give unmistakable definition to the rear end (modern technology would probably see instead a "light bar" in the slim area along the rear fenders and lower deck). This is the only closed Chrysler except the "letter series" worth over $10,000 in show-winning condition. Badge at roof quarter reads "LeBaron Coachwork."

The reasons for its marketing failure are not complex. Imperial constantly suffered from an identity crisis, being called a "Chrysler" even after millions of dollars of advertising had been spent to establish it as separate marque. Its identity was not aided when it gradually became more and more like the Chrysler New Yorker as the sixties went by. Imperial never had a product to excite the public imagination like the 1961 and subsequent Lincoln Continentals. Finally, in a market dominated by Cadillac, even Lincoln was destined to be an also-ran; there just weren't that many non-Cadillac customers in the luxury car field.

Before Virgil Exner left Chrysler as chief of design, he had envisioned a completely new, Imperial for 1962, resembling his 1962 Dodges and Plymouths. That this didn't reach production is fortunate. The production '62s were modestly but deftly facelifted; the fins were shorn down to nubs of what they'd been. The new, elongated bullet taillights were freestanding, but blended better with the rear renders than the earlier bombsight versions. Sales improved in 1962.

Another mild facelift ensured for 1963, comprising a new grille composed of elongated rectangles, a crisp new roofline, and a restyled rear deck with the taillights integrated into the fender tips. Production remained about the same.

Elwood Engel's stylists took over and squared off the silhouette for 1964, producing an Imperial very reminiscent of the Continental Engel had styled for Ford, its fenderlines traced in brightwork. The low-selling Imperial Custom line was dropped, and pillarless body styles were no longer called "Southamptons." Though this pared the line down to only five models, sales were extremely good at 23,000 for the model year, a performance that would not be approached again until 1969.

Engel stood mainly pat for 1965; the only significant change was a new grille with glass-enclosed headlamps. At the New York Automobile Show, Imperial displayed an exotic showcar, the LeBaron D'Or, which used gold striping and embellishments and was painted a special gold fleck, "Royal Essence Laurel Gold," which sounds like a strip artist but was really very tasteful. The '66s were again changed very little, but did receive a new 440ci V-8; sales, however, were disappointing.

By 1967, Chrysler engineers had had enough experience with unit construction to be satisfied with this approach for Imperial. Cynics might say it also saved the company a lot of money to build Imperial the same way it built its Chrysler models, but vast technical improvements had occurred over the years, allowing unit bodies to be computer-tested for strength before any given shape was finalized. Unibody construction also cut weight by about 100lb. The '67s were therefore all-new and completely restyled, the last serious effort to garner de-cent volume. Sales did improve, but only slightly, and the 1968 Imperial, a modest facelift, was the last distinctly different car to bear that distinguished name. The '68s also saw the last of the Crown convertibles. From 1969 on, Imperials would share their sheet-metal with Chrysler, and as such, they will be left to a later chapter.

Identification

1962: Freestanding headlamps were retained; long, freestanding taillamps mounted at the tops of the rear fenders were new.

1963: Squared off roofline, new complicated grille made up of repeated small rectangles with an

For 1963 they chopped the bullet taillights and built modest lenses into the fender tips, but lost all definition in the process; from the back this Custom four-door hardtop looks like an oversized Valiant.

Engel's square look first arrived at Chrysler Corporation on the 1964 Imperial. The Crown Coupe sold for $5,800 and is worth $7,500 today in top condition.

A new fine-mesh grille and glass covered headlights marked the otherwise almost unchanged 1965 Imperials, the last to employ the efficient 413 engine.

"eagle" badge in the center; taillights inset into rear fenders. Freestanding headlamps retained.

1964: Very square profile with "formal" roofline; freestanding headlamps dropped and a divided grille applied.

1965: New fine mesh grille with glass covered headlamps.

1966: Cross-hatched grille, with each square housing the familiar elongated rectangles. Dummy spare tire outline removed from rear deck; back-up lights inset in rear bumpers. Larger engine.

1967: Unibody construction brought a new look: sharp front fenders housing parking lights; new style grille with prominent nameplate, flanked by integrated quad headlamps; vertical rear bumpers and horizontal "character lines" along the bodysides.

1968: New grille extending around the front end to enclose the parking and cornering lights; dual moldings on lower bodysides; rear side market lights. Narrow paint stripes along the beltline.

Appraisal

Imperials in this period have appreciated at about the same rate as New Yorkers. Convertibles

Only about 500 1966 Crown convertibles were built, and the best ones can bring over $15,000 nowadays, though "condition 3" cars are worth only a third or so as much. New grille with square sectors was the chief styling change; note factory-issue three-stripe whitewalls.

"Imperial is always new," said the promotion for 1967, which saw the broadest design changes in ten years. Imperial had finally adopted Unibody construction. Top of the line as usual was the LeBaron four-door hardtop, but these cars do not command the high prices paid for pre-1967 LeBarons.

The last Imperial convertible, 1968, is desirable for that fact and its crisp, clean styling. Fewer than 500 were built, which makes them rare today. The '68s are immediately distinguished by front and rear side marker lights and thin-bar horizontal frontispiece.

are, as usual, much more desirable than closed body styles and, being much scarcer, have reached relatively high prices. By every collector yardstick I consulted, the '62 (and lookalike '63 is the pick of the litter. It has all the traditional Virgil Exner flash of the best-known early Imperials, with enough new features to attract the collector's eye: its combination of modest tailfins, elongated "bombsight" taillamps, freestanding headlamps, and extensive glass area seem to appeal more than succeeding models. If you have a choice between a '62/'63 and some later vintage in equal condition, choose the '62/'63 every time. Above all, check these cars carefully for rust and the condition of hard to find body parts, like freestanding headlamps. They'll cost the world to repair or replace, assuming you are able to locate them.

Summary and Prospects

There doesn't seem to be much going on among Imperials with the automotive investor crowd. Production figures were extremely low (just look at some of them!) so on paper you'd think they'd be worth more. But Imperials never enjoyed the incredible highs of tailfinned Cadillacs from the same period, and they remain among the most affordable sixties collector cars today. You'd be hard-pressed, in fact, to find a convertible priced at $20,000, and the consensus is that the '62/'63 is the only one that might be worth that much, presuming it was a perfect show-winning restoration or a mint original. The prices below, which are for "condition 1" cars, mean that you can find a big Imp ragtop for as little as $10,000 or $12,000 if you're willing to accept a little wear and tear. Bottom line: like most other Chryslers from the sixties other than the "letter series" 300s, these are good, sound collector cars but not "investments." If return on capital expenditure is your aim, get a "letter series" or a

Specifications

Engines (net hp)
Type: cast-iron V-8
413.0ci (4.18 x 3.75in), 340hp (1962-65)
440.0ci (4.32 x 3.75in), 350hp (1966-68), 360 (1968 with dual exhaust)

Chassis and Drivetrain
Separate chassis frame (1962-66) unit body and frame (1967-68); shaft drive, four-wheel hydraulic brakes, steel wheels. TorqueFlite automatic transmission standard.

Size and Weight
Wheelbase (in):
129in (1962-66), 127in (1967-68)
Curb Weight (lb):
1962-63 4,600-4,800lb; 1964-65 5,000-5,200lb; 1966 4,900-5,100lb; 1967-68 4,800-4,900lb

Town & Country woody.

Return on investment (95-point condition 1):

	1980	1995	*Return
1962-68 Crown sedans/ coupes	$2,500	$7,000	7.1%
1962 Crown convertible	$5,000	$20,000	9.7%
1963 Crown convertible	$4,500	$17,000	9.3%
1962 LeBaron	$3,500	$10,000	7.3%
1963-68 LeBaron	$3,000	$9,000	7.6%
1964-68 Crown convertible	$4,250	$16,000	9.3%

*compound annual rate of return unadjusted for maintenance, insurance, and running costs

Production

	1962	1963	1964	1965	1966
Custom hardtop, 2dr.	826	749	0	0	0
Custom hardtop, 4dr.	4,620	3,264	0	0	0
Crown hardtop, 2dr.	1,010	1,067	5,233	3,974	2,373
Crown hardtop, 4dr.	6,911	6,960	14,181	11,628	8,977
Crown convertible	554	531	922	633	514
LeBaron hardtop, 4dr.	1,449	1,537	2,949	2,164	1,878

	1967	1968
Crown hardtop, 2dr.	3,235	2,656
Crown hardtop, 4dr.	9,415	8,492
Crown sedan, 4dr.	2,193	1,887
Crown convertible	577	474
LeBaron hardtop, 4dr.	2,194	1,852

Chapter 22

Newport & New Yorker
1972-78

The 1970 model year had seen the last big Chrysler convertible and 1971 was the last year for "fuselage styling," although the 1972-73 models continued to be based on the 1969 shell. Styling remained clean, even if easy-change items like grilles, taillights, and side decoration became a bit more tacky with time. A new engine more adaptable to emissions requirements than the old 383 was introduced for 1973, and the smaller 360 was dropped from the Newport Royal. Electronic ignition was now standard. New Yorkers retained the big-block 440 with added emission controls.

The one-millionth Chrysler came down the Jefferson Avenue lines on June 26, 1973, a Newport sedan, which by then was the base model, since the Newport Royal disappeared the previous year. All '73s used new sheetmetal, and the bumper-framed grille gave way to a more conventional front end with bulkier bumpers, in line with federal impact regulations.

Chrysler was still plugging the big car in 1974, but sales sank in the wake of the energy crisis. Still riding a 124in platform, about 5in shorter overall and

bearing a crisp new look, Chryslers wore pseudo-classic square grilles of the sort they'd avoided when this fad arrived in the early 1970s. Engine options and horsepower were down. The line-up consisted of Newport, New Yorker, and Town & Country.

Few at Chrysler had foreseen the energy crisis, which accelerated buyer resistance to big cars that had been building anyway because of galloping sticker prices. Sales of the record-priced 1975s dropped to 1970 levels, and a two-month backlog of unsold cars quickly piled up. Chrysler chairman Lynn Townsend refused to slash prices. Instead he slashed production. By early November 1974, Chrysler sales were down 34 percent. The result was employee layoffs and 300,000 unsold cars by early 1975. Chrysler now began instituting cash rebates, something the industry had never done before. Hard times caused a rethink: it was now no longer inconceivable that "there will never be a small Chrysler."

The first sign of a change of heart was the 1975 Cordoba (Chapter 24), and the second was the 1977 LeBaron, Chrysler's first genuinely small car. There were changes in mind for the bread-and-butter Newport and New Yorker, too, but given industry lead times, these would have to wait until 1979.

The 1975-78 big Chryslers therefore remained much the same as they had. The accent was now

For the middle seventies, the last really huge Chryslers continued to garner sales, surviving the fuel crisis and becoming in the end one of the few options for buyers of traditional "standard size" American cars. This is a 1973 New Yorker with the 440 engine standard.

The smooth, "fuselage styling" that had been Chrysler's forté since 1969 is apparent on this 1972 Newport coupe, which sold for $4,400.

Brougham was now the only version of New Yorker, although a deluxe St. Regis package (road wheels, interior upgrades) was optional. The grille bore a

strong resemblance to Mercedes-Benz's. A Brougham St. Regis (padded top) coupe and standard four-door hardtop are shown.

less on performance and more on luxury—combined with efficiency. The most opulent model was the New Yorker Brougham, an Imperial without the name, the luxury leader after 1975. Boasting standard leather, velour, or brocade upholstery, shag carpeting, imitation walnut trim, and filigree moldings, it was a floating bordello of a car, yet remarkably economical. Aiming to lower its corporate average fleet economy (CAFE), Chrysler had fitted a numerically lower final drive ratio and offered the optional "Fuel Pacer," an intake manifold pressure sensor connected to a warning light that glowed a warning to heavy-footed use of the accelerator.

If Town & Country's day was done (it was dropped after 1977) the Newport and New Yorker gradually recovered popularity: moreso, in the New Yorker Brougham's case. Chrysler sold close to 80,000 in 1977—they remained unabashedly big cars, and with Ford and GM building fewer and fewer cars that size there was good reason to keep building them. Despite a truncated line of Newports, the behemoths still managed over 80,000 sales in 1978, their final year. Chrysler would have kept them in the line were it not for the inexorable CAFE regulations; they hated to see them go. But this, of course, was the "old" Chrysler Corporation. Today you wouldn't catch Chrysler people even thinking about cars this big.

Identification

1972: Fuselage styling; heavy chrome bumper-grille retained from 1971, but divided in the center, resulting in two grille inserts.

1973: Newport Royal dropped. Combination bumper-grille gave way to a conventional low-mounted bumper under a squared off grille flanked by quad headlights, looking all to much like a

For 1976, the New Yorker Brougham took over from Imperial, retaining the Imperial's grille. The standard interior was velour cloth over deep contoured foam cushioning, finished with leather and vinyl.

Chevy Impala. New Yorker carried heavier side trim and different taillights.

1974: A restyle with minor downsizing, slightly narrower, and 5in shorter than 1973. Newport grille cross hatched; New Yorker grille contained a double stack of rectangular shapes and full length lower body rub-rail.

1975: Oblong openings in front bumper, Mercedes-like grillework. The Brougham was now the only version of the New Yorker, although an upscale St. Regis trim package was offered.

1976: New Yorker brougham now resembled the 1975 Imperial, with a bold, upright, vertical bar grille flanked by hidden headlamps; Newport had a conventional grille with many tiny rectangles flanked by uncovered quad headlamps. Newport

Optional interiors on the 1976 Newport: a touch of tradition in the Highlander plaid cloth/vinyl package

on a four-door hardtop, and striking "Castilian" cloth on a four-door sedan.

Custom grille was Mercedes-like with two prominent horizontal bars and one vertical set against a small meshwork.

1977: A facelift with crisper, squarer lines; Mercedes-like grille on Newport resembled last year's Newport Custom, which had now been eliminated. New Yorker Brougham continued with very little change.

1978: Segmented vertical grillework on New Yorker Brougham. Newport pillared sedan was dropped; appearance of pillarless models changed little. Lean Burn 400ci V-8 was now standard on both Newport and New Yorker.

Appraisal
The more luxury the better on these cars: collectors

Above and opposite page
A solid customer base still preferred the big, luxurious New Yorkers as the seventies drew to a

close. This silver St. Regis coupe carried optional red leather upholstery and a dash with simulated rosewood.

The 1977 Town & Country was the last of Chrysler's jumbo wagons, priced now at close to $7,000. You can buy the best one in the world now for about half that. As always, six- and nine-passenger seating was available, the latter via a rear-facing rear seat.

who want them (who aren't many) look for New Yorkers with the St. Regis package, and definitely prefer the 1976-78 New Yorker Brougham (an Imperial in all but name) to lesser models. Coupes have a very slight edge in value over four-door models, and four-door hardtops are a shade more desirable than four-door sedans (which petered out in 1976). There are certain remarkably low production figures, especially for Town & Country wagons, but nobody cares; these are not high-demand Chryslers.

Summary and Prospects

All our survey of 1980 vs. 1995 values tells us is that fine original examples of these cars stopped depreciating in the early 1980s and are now increasing (modestly) in value. But that's true of almost any production car in better-than-average condition that manages to survive fifteen years or so. Certainly

none of these big Chryslers has shown any significant investor potential. I know several collectors who keep a New Yorker Brougham around for occasional summertime travel, a kind of nostalgic artifact of a class of car that is gone and will never return. Nostalgia value aside, there's not much to recommend these cars except luxury and sheer size; yet undeniably they exert a certain influence.

Return on investment (95-point condition 1):

	1980	1995	*Return
1972-75 Newport hardtop, 2dr.	$1,800	$4,500	6.3%
1972-75 Newport 4dr. models	$1,900	$3,500	4.2%
1976-78 Newport (all models)	**	$4,000	n/a
1972-75 New Yorker (all models)	$2,000	$4,500	5.6%
1972-77 Town & Country wagons	$1,750	$4,000	5.7%
1976-78 New Yorker Brougham	**	$5,000	n/a

*compound annual rate of return unadjusted for maintenance, insurance, and running costs
**still depreciating in 1980

Production

	1972	1973	1974	1975
Newport hardtop, 2dr.*	22,622	27,456	13,784	10,485
Newport sedan, 4dr.*	47,437	54,147	26,944	26,944
Newport hardtop, 4dr.*	15,1852	0,175	8,968	8,968
Newport Custom hardtop, 2dr.	10,326	12,293	7,206	5,831
Newport Custom sedan, 4dr.	19,278	20,092	10,569	9,623
Newport Custom hardtop, 4dr.	15,457	20,050	9,892	11,626
Town & Country wagon, 6pass.	6,473	5,353	2,236	1,891
Town & Country wagon, 9pass.	14,116	14,687	5,958	4,764
New Yorker hardtop, 2dr.	5,567	0	0	0
New Yorker sedan, 4dr.	7,296	7,991	3,072	0
New Yorker hardtop, 4dr.	10,013	7,619	3,066	0
New Yorker Brougham hardtop, 2dr.	4,635	9,190	7,980	7,567
New Yorker Brougham sedan, 4dr.	5,971	8,541	4,533	5,698
New Yorker Brougham hardtop, 4dr.	20,328	26,635	13,165	12,775

* Newport Royal in 1972 only

	1976	1977	1978
Newport hardtop, 2dr.	6,109	16,227	8,877
Newport sedan, 4dr.	16,3703	9,424	0
Newport hardtop, 4dr.	5,908	20,738	30,078
Newport Custom hardtop, 2dr.	6,448	0	0
Newport Custom sedan, 4dr.	11,587	0	0
Newport Custom hardtop, 4dr.	9,893	0	0
Town & Country wagon, 6pass.	1,770	2,488	0
Town & Country wagon, 9pass.	3,769	6,081	0
New Yorker Brougham hardtop, 2dr.	11,510	19,732	11,469
New Yorker Brougham hardtop, 4dr.	28,327	56,610	33,090

Specifications
Engines (nethp)
Cast-iron V-8, 360.0ci (4.00 x 3.58lb):
155hp: optional 1977 Newport, all 1978s
170/175hp: 1972 Royal
180/190hp: optional 1975-76 Newport and all 1978s
Cast-iron V-8, 400.0ci (4.34 x 3.38lb):
175/195hp: 1975-76 Newport, optional 1975-76 NY Brougham
185hp: 1973-74 Newport
190hp: 1972 Newport, T&C, optional Royal; 1977 Newport, optional T&C, New Yorker; 1978 Newport, New Yorker
205hp: optional 1974 Newport 210hp: optional all 1976s
Cast-iron V-8, 440.0ci (4.32 x 3.75lb):
185/195hp: optional 1978 Newport, New Yorker
195 nethp: 1977 T&C, New Yorker, optional Newport
205hp: 1976 T&C, New Yorker, optional Newport
215 nethp: 1973 T&C, New Yorker, optional Newport; 1975 T&C, New Yorker, optional Newport
225hp: 1972 New Yorker)
230hp: 1974 T&C, New Yorker
260hp: optional 1975 NY Brougham
275hp: optional 1974 New Yorker

Chassis and Drivetrain
Unit body and frame, four-wheel hydraulic brakes, steel wheels. TorqueFlite automatic transmission standard.

Size and Weight
Wheelbase (in):
124in; 1972 Town & Country 122in
Curb Weight (lb):
Newport 4,000-4,500lb; New Yorker 4,300-4,800lb; Town & Country 4,600-5,100lb

★★★

Chapter 23

Imperial
1969-75

"Anybody can cheapen a name," said James Nance, the last president of independent Packard: "it's the easiest thing in the world." In 1969 Chrysler began doing to the Imperial what Packard had done to its senior models about thirty years before. For the first time in almost a generation, the Imperial shared Chrysler's sheetmetal. The new look and a lower priced LeBaron temporarily paid off, but in the longer term Chrysler was left with an Imperial that just looked like a Chrysler. This resurrected the Imp's age old identity problem. Similarly, the decision to build the junior Packard One Twenty had diminished the lust for all-out luxury Packards thirty-four years earlier.

In product planning, too, Imperial designers didn't anticipate changing public tastes. By the 1970s those tastes increasingly caused buyers to look for "compact luxury cars," built in places other than Detroit, and Chrysler (like GM and Ford for a time) had no answer for them. By the mid-seventies, when the market for land yachts had diminished appreciably, Chrysler simply gave Imperial the axe, while Cadillac slapped its nameplate on a near-compact, called it the Seville, and made a virtue of smallness. (Chrysler tried this too, but only as a reaction to its competition in 1977, and chose the wrong name (LeBaron). What they should have done was brought out a new, compact, ultra-luxury Imperial.

But hindsight is cheap, and far too easily indulged . . .

The 1969-70 Chrysler-based Imperials were the cleanest in history, with long, low "fuselage styling," a full-width egg-crate grille, concealed headlamps, and sequential turn signals set into the rear bumper. Ventless side glass was a feature of air conditioned coupes. Although the 127in wheelbase was retained, the new body stretched overall length by 5in, yet curb weight was about 100lb less. The engine, as before, was the 350hp 440. A hardtop coupe and sedan were offered in both Crown and LeBaron trim, plus a pillared Crown sedan priced identically with the Crown hardtop. LeBaron was no longer the $7,000 semi-custom it had been in past years, and its list price was down around $800

from 1968. Combined sales of the two LeBarons exceeded those of the Crown for the first time: a genuine boost to sales, which topped 22,000 in 1969, the third best year in Imperial history. That was the best year, and the last really good year. From 1970, the Imperial trundled toward oblivion.

The '70 models were a repeat of 1969s, but the public had overindulged the year before and bought barely 11,000 of them. For 1971 the Crown was dropped, leaving the LeBaron as the only Imperial ("Imperial by Chrysler") in the line and priced at increasingly higher levels. The Bendix anti-skid brake system, a $250 option exclusive to Imperial for 1971, was extended to the entire Chrysler line for 1972.

The '72s had crisper lines and a bold upright bumper/grille, plus a 3in-shorter wheelbase and 100lb less weight, all commendable improvements.

Looking more like a Chrysler than at any time since 1954, the 1969 Imperial was "fuselage styled" and distinguished mainly by its unique full-width grille with hidden headlamps. The 127in wheelbase was slightly longer than Chrysler's, and the list price was higher. Late model Imperials do not really attract many collectors.

With a deck large enough to land a Piper Cub, the '70 was altered only in detail. Sales fell off drastically, and this LeBaron coupe accounted for only 1,803.

But these modest reductions had nothing to do with the fuel shortage, which Chrysler hadn't anticipated, and were really inevitable given the continued use of Chrysler sheetmetal. The 1973 model with its thin horizontal grille was a cleaner looking car, marred by "5mph bumpers"; what really did it in, though, was the "energy crisis" of late 1973 and 1974. By the time that was over, cars like the Imperial were largely considered dinosaurs. The adoption of a handsome new front end with square

A full-width egg-crate grille, and the Imperial name replaced by the familiar eagle badge, marked up-front changes to the LeBaron coupe for 1972.

grille and hidden headlamps wasn't enough to stem the nationwide desertion of full-size cars, and fewer than 10,000 Imperials were sold in the final model year of 1975. The last of the line, a LeBaron four-door hardtop, left the Jefferson Avenue, Detroit plant on June 12, 1975, bearing serial number YM43-T5C-182947.

Identification

1969: Chrysler-like "fuselage styling" with sheer sides, horizontal taillights built into rear bumper, and combination bumper/grille consisting of fine vertical and horizontal bars with two prominent central horizontal bars. LeBarons had vinyl padded roof, "formal" (oval) rear window, cloth and leather bench seats, and storage compartments in all doors.

1970: Headlamps were hidden behind a full-width grid pattern grille and large oblong side marker lights were on front fenders ahead of the wheel wells. LeBaron features as 1969.

1971: The Crown series was dropped, leaving only the LeBaron. Cross hatched grille contains rectangular headlight doors; Imperial name spelled out in individual letters on leading edge of hood; front marker lights had clear and amber sections.

1972: Imperial name on hood replaced by central stylized eagle badge; full width cross hatched grille with headlamps completely hidden.

1973: Vertical front bumper guards, grille composed of very thin horizontal blades.

1974: New square grille, slightly vee'd, composed of six sections of vertical blades; headlamp doors hide the headlights. Wrap-around front signal lights. The Crown Coupe package, on two-door hardtops only, included opera windows and a vinyl covered front roof section.

1975: Deeper dish wheel covers; body styling unchanged from 1974.

Appraisal

There is a slight edge for the two-door model over the four-door; no discernible difference exists between LeBarons and Crowns in the 1969-70 model years—apparently the scarcity of the Crown is balanced by the greater luxury of the LeBaron. Collectors seem to prefer the earlier Imperials, which is curious considering the low production of the later ones.

Summary and Prospects

Like the concurrent New Yorkers and Newports, Imperials from this period stopped depreciating in the 1980s, but are worth no more than any well preserved older car today. Our figures are for "condition 1" vehicles; hence it ought to be possible to obtain a decent example for under $4,000.

Last of the first: the final Imperial built as a separate make coming off the production line on June 12th, 1975. Priced at $10,403.35, this LeBaron bears VIN #YM43-T5CX-182947. Does any reader know where it is today?

There is no indication of any upward movement among these later Imperials in the foreseeable future; they'll be lucky to keep pace with the inflation rate.

Return on investment (95-point condition 1):

	1980	1995	Return
1969-70 hardtop, 2dr.	$2,200	$6,500	7.5%
1969-70 hardtop, 4dr.	$2,000	$5,500	7.0%
1971-72 hardtop, 2dr.	$2,700	$6,000	5.5%
1971-72 hardtop, 4dr.	$2,500	$5,500	5.4%
1973-75 hardtop, 2dr.	**	$4,500	n/a
1974 Crown Coupe	**	$5,000	n/a
1973-75 hardtop, 4dr.	**	$4,000	n/a

*compound annual rate of return unadjusted for maintenance, insurance, and running costs
**still depreciating in 1980

Production

	1969	1970
Crown hardtop, 2dr.	224	254
Crown hardtop, 4dr.	823	1,330
Crown sedan, 4dr.	1,617	0
LeBaron hardtop, 2dr.	4,592	1,803
LeBaron hardtop, 4dr.	14,82	18,426

	1971	1972	1973	1974	1975
LeBaron hardtop, 2dr.	1,442	2,332	2,563	3,850	2,728
LeBaron hardtop, 4dr.	10,116	13,472	14,166	10,576	6,102

★

Chapter 24

Cordoba
1975-83

Some cars, like the 1955 Imperials, seem to look better as they age, while others just look common. The Cordoba strikes me as one of the latter. Although it was greeted by loud huzzahs, and had a certain Jaguar-esque look, it now seems so dated (long hood, blunt grille, short deck, rear drive, no room in the back) that it doesn't bear a second glance. Yet there are certain Cordobas and Cordoba-variations that are definitely collectible. Maybe it's just that

I've seen so many rotted out, tail-dragging Cordobas around the roads of New England that my brain has numbed to the species.

The Cordoba, which originally was to have been a Plymouth, clearly broke new ground for Chrysler, which had never built a "personal luxury" coupe before. But like most things from Highland Park in the 1970s, it was an echo not a choice: a backhanded reaction to competitive pressures.

"The New, Small Chrysler," an unabashed sop to the personal luxury car market which Chrysler should have entered years before, Cordoba debuted in 1975. Front end with small inboard driving lights was reminiscent of Jaguar, while the rest looked like a Chevy Montecarlo, unfortunately. Elaborate interior and comfort options were stressed over performance; though engines up to 400ci were available, all were detuned and net horsepower was 235 at best. From 1980, some Cordobas were equipped with six-cylinder engines.

Thunderbird and the Buick Riviera had more or less created the "personal luxury" concept in the early sixties; Chevrolet extended the idea down-market with the Montecarlo, while Lincoln pushed it up into the ultra-luxury field with its Continental Marks. The only piece of this idea Chrysler Corporation had in the sixties was the Dodge Charger, and that had really been more hot rod than a Chrysler version of the T-bird.

In 1975, though, designers created a new Charger with the emphasis on luxury, and it was logical to product-plan a Chrysler version of it. The Cordoba had a definite frontal resemblance to Jaguar's XJ6, and looked like a cross between the Jag and a Montecarlo. This wasn't necessarily bad; the Cordoba was a good product in its day. The 115in wheelbase was the shortest on any Chrysler since before World War II, and only 2.5in longer than on the first car to bear the badge, way back in 1924.

Chrysler's promise never to build a small car thus lasted only fifteen years. The Cordoba was blatantly advertised as "the new small Chrysler," and pushed as a kind of gran turismo—which it wasn't, standard steel-belted radial tires and anti-sway bars notwithstanding. Reflecting the car's true character, power seats, windows, and door locks were optional, and interiors were beautifully upholstered in crushed velour or brocade cloth and vinyl. Available at extra cost, introduced by the dulcet tones of Ricardo Montalban, was "rich Corinthian leather."

Whether the leather came from Corinth was a question, but it sounded terrific. Standard power was the 360 V-8 in its mildest form, but since Cordobas aimed at a wide variety of customer, engines as small as the 318 and as big as the 440 were also available. The package certainly worked: Chrysler sold 120,000 Cordobas in its first year, and in 1977 hit the record with over 180,000.

A T-bar roof with removable tinted glass panels was new in 1977, as was a manual sunroof. A Cordoba "S" model, priced $200 lower than the regular coupe, was added in 1978, when stacked quad headlights gave it more than ever the look of a Chevy Montecarlo. More interesting was the "Cordoba 300" for 1979, with a blacked-out cross-bar grille, a clear nostalgia trip to the old letter series 300s. The $2040 300 package also included red leather bucket seats; red, white, and blue bodyside moldings; and a Spinnaker white paint job (the only

One of the best looking late Cordobas was the 1981 model, with handsome vinyl padded rear quarter windows and optional wire wheel covers. A direct crib of the Mark Cross Continental Mark VI was the Cabriolet Roof Two-Tone Package, which included a sailcloth textured convertible-like roof treatment and Pearl White/Nightwatch Blue paint combination. The Cabriolet Roof without two-toning was also available.

The base Cordoba by 1982 had become very ordinary looking; more interesting was the Cordoba LS with a slope-back front end, a grille reminiscent of the old 300s, and a Cabriolet Roof option.

color available). Although it had a firm suspension, leather-wrapped steering wheel, engine-turned dashboard with full instruments, and GR60x15 Aramid-belted tires, it was still a product of its time, powered by the anemic 195hp 360 V-8. "Crown" (half padded vinyl) and landau roofs were also available, with two-tone paint jobs, but only 693 Crown roofs were ordered in 1979.

The next generation Cordoba arrived on the LeBaron compact platform for 1980, 6in shorter, 4in narrower, and available for the first time with a six-cylinder engine. More crisply styled, it was more a sporty LeBaron coupe than an individual personal-luxury car, and sales, which had leveled off in 1979 dropped to only a few more than 50,000.

There are several interesting permutations worth looking for among the later Cordobas. The Cordoba Crown, as before, included a padded landau-style vinyl half roof, meeting the rear painted roof section with a brushed aluminum border. It had opera windows and inset backlight with no exposed moldings and special wheel covers. The Crown Corinthian edition had similar roof treatment with black walnut metallic or cream-on-beige paint treatment; the black walnut job used pseudo-lizardskin for its vinyl top and gold accent stripes, while the cream-and-beige version had "Laredo grain" vinyl and beige accents. Corinthians also came with special identification, leather-wrapped tilt steering wheel, dual chrome remote rearview mirrors, intermittent wipers, whitewalls, and special wheel covers.

Sales were now becoming almost academic, and when Lee Iacocca stepped in to rescue Chrysler, the Cordoba's days were definitely numbered. A sharp-looking 1981-82 LS model, priced some $1,000 before the standard Cordoba, was an attractive package, especially in 1982 with its 300-like cross-bar grille and raked back front end; these models were, however, scarce on the ground. Fewer than 15,000 Cordobas were sold in 1983, their last year.

Identification

1975: Grille composed of three tiers of small oblong sections arranged vertically; grille continued into top of bumper. Large round outer headlamps with smaller inboard headlamps in the style of Jaguar XJ6.

1976: Fine mesh vertical bar grille continued under bumper.

1977: Grille had a fine crosshatch pattern dominated by vertical bars, repeated in top of bumper.

1978: Quad headlamps stacked vertically, plainer mesh grille. Lower priced Cordoba "S" added.

1979: Bold vertically textured grille with thin vertical strips and heavy frame surround. Cordoba 300 added with standard white paint job, red leather buckets, and letter series style red, white, and blue striping.

1980: LeBaron body with shorter wheelbase, single recessed rectangular headlamps, vertically ribbed square grille. Unlike the LeBaron with its high-mounted horizontal parking lights, Cordoba parking lights were vertical and mounted inboard of the headlamps. Franklin Mint supplied "coin" medallions for front fenders and hood ornament.

1981: Little change from 1980; high-strength steel bumpers and a sporty LS model with "soft" front end were added.

1982: "Coin" medallions dropped, padded vinyl roof and halogen headlamps standard. LS had a slanted front end with 300-like crossbar grille.

1983: Front marker lights were now all-amber instead of amber and clear; Chrysler Pentastar stand-up hood ornament was new. LS model dropped.

Appraisal

Cordobas are complicated machines and it doesn't pay to invest in a basket case, or even a well worn one: go for the mint-low mileage original. Among these, obviously the 1979 Cordoba 300 is the best choice. It will set you back more, but it's gaining in value at double the rate of other models on the strength of its throwback 300 letter series styling; one 300 collector I know actually considers his Cordoba 300 an extension of the species, but drawing that conclusion takes a lot of enthusiasm. Next in the collector hierarchy are the 1977-79 models with T-bar roof.

Summary and Prospects

Cordobas in fine condition have stopped depreciating, and in a few more years will be worth what they sold for new (not allowing for inflation).

Specifications

Engines (net hp)

Six, 225ci (3.40 x 3.12in), 85/90hp (std Six 1980-83)
V-8, 318ci (3.91 x 3.31in), 135-150hp (optional 1975-78, std 1979) same, 120/130hp (std V-8 1980-83); 165hp (opt 1981-82)
V-8, 360ci (4.00 x 3.58in), 170/180hp (std 1975, opt 1976-78) same, 150/155hp (std 1978, opt 1977/79); 195hp (opt 1979, std on 1980 Cordoba 300)
V-8, 400ci (4.34 x 3.38in), 190/210hp (std 1977, optional 1975-76 and 1978-79) same, 175hp (std 1976); 235/240hp (opt 1975-76)
V-8, 440ci (4.32 x 3.75in), 215/260hp (opt 1975); 195/205hp (opt 1976-77)

Chassis and Drivetrain

Unit body and frame; shaft drive, four-wheel hydraulic brakes, steel wheels. TorqueFlite automatic transmission standard.

Size and Weight

Wheelbase (in): 1975-79 115.0in; 1980-83 112.7in
Curb Weight (lb): 1975-78 4,000lb; 1979 3,700-3,900lb 1980-83 3,200-3,500lb

The last Cordobas continued to stress the formal luxury style, and could hardly be called performance cars with only the 318ci V-8 or, more shocking, a Slant Six (available 1980-83). Whether these plug-ordinary Cordobas will ever seriously be collected is a question; a mint original might be a good buy for transportation, but don't look for appreciation.

The Cordoba 300, which cost close to $8,000 in 1979, can still be had for well under that. The change in values of earlier models since 1987 is modest but undeniably upward. Don't look for very rapid gains in the next ten years, but expect condition 1 and 2 cars to cost more each year as time goes by. As to the LeBaron-based 1980-83 models, it's too soon to tell, but it would seem logical that they will continue to gain in value at about the same rate as the earlier versions. There was also a novel "Cabriolet" roof option which made the Cordoba look like a convertible, with fabric-like canvas top and blind rear quarters.

Return on investment (95-point condition 1):

	1987	1995	*Return
1975-79 Cordoba	$4,500	$4,900	1.1%
1979 Cordoba 300	$5,000	$6,000	2.3%
1980-83 Cordoba V-8	**	$6,000	n/a
1980-83 Cordoba Six	**	$5,000	n/a

*compound annual rate of return unadjusted for maintenance, insurance, and running costs
** still depreciating

Production

	1975	1976	1977	1978	1979
coupe	150,105	120,462	183,146	124,825	84,204
300 coupe	0	0	0	0	3,811

	1980	1981	1982	1983
coupe	26,333	11,646	10,150	12,572
Cabriolet coupe	*	1,332	1,612	899
LS coupe	3,252	7,315	3,136	0
Crown coupe	14,752	*	0	0
Crown Corinthian	2,069	1,957	0	0

*included in coupe figures

Chapter 25

Chrysler Imperial
1981-83

One hopes that Imperial, a distinguished name, is not gone forever. Ostensibly its image of gargantuan size and tailfinned extravagance is out of sync with the present-day Chrysler concept of swift, aerodynamic, egg-shaped grand touring cars thinly disguised as family sedans. But the Imperial's history goes back far beyond the Exner era to almost the first years of the marque. Throughout its lifetime, the name Imperial stood for the best Chrysler in the line-up. Why couldn't it be applied, for example, to an extended wheelbase version of the LHS?

Imperial's last appearance to date was in the early 1990s as a glorified K-car, about which the less said the better. Its penultimate appearance, and the subject of this chapter, was as a high-priced personal luxury coupe designed to compete with the Continental Mark and Cadillac Eldorado. A striking, knife-edged coupe with a raked-back front end and a grille clearly inspired by Continentals, it arrived in 1981, selling for just under $20,000. Its classic-era bustle-back trunk was de-

rived from that of the Cadillac Seville (which had just ditched that styling as passé—Chrysler Design was reacting again. Still, fifteen years ago you'd have thought Chrysler could sell a car like this. They didn't: barely 7,000 went out the door in the Imperial's first year, and production for the next twenty-four months was negligible.

It was a lot of car for the money. Based on the Cordoba, the Imperial had its own unique styling, and though the bustle back was out of proportion the overall impression was quite good. There was a massive selection of audio equipment, the only extra-cost option was a $1,044 power moonroof, and customers could specify clearcoat paint jobs, digital electronic instrumentation, and a Mark Cross leather or cloth interior at no extra cost. There was no power—nothing had much power in 1981—but the thing was certainly luxurious, and engineers had taken pains to minimize the occupants from noise, billing the Imperial as "the quietest car in Chrysler history." The use of

Revived after a five-year absence, Imperial for 1981 was a personal luxury coupe with high emphasis on quality of fit and finish and a no-charge two-year, 30,000-mile warranty. Styling was neo-classic in the Cadillac Seville idiom; but hold your finger over the enormous bustle-back—wouldn't a sheer fastback have looked much better?

Imperial features included high fashion accents in crystal and leather, the latest in electronic instrumentation and fuel injection. One price bought all: the only option was a moonroof.

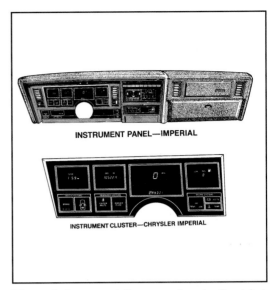

INSTRUMENT PANEL—IMPERIAL

INSTRUMENT CLUSTER—CHRYSLER IMPERIAL

Goodyear Arriva tires with low rolling resistance, plus exceptional attention to insulation and sound deadening, were the keys to this claim. Some of the Imperial's accouterments, like the crystal hood ornament and optional "Frank Sinatra package" (special ID with a batch of Blue Eyes' tapes) were distinctly tacky, but since when did tackiness fail to help sell cars?

Somehow, though, the new Imperial bombed. The market for big, thirsty coupes that essentially were two-seaters had disappeared; even Cadillac had downsized and refined the Eldorado. Had Chrysler built this car in 1970, things might have been different.

The 1982 version was the same car with a $3,000 higher price, which of course cost Chrysler even more money in the long run. In 1983 they cut the price down toward its 1981 level, but the damage was done and the public wasn't having any. Be-

Electronic instrumentation proved a shortlived fad: there's really nothing to compare with the communication of range and reserves of analog instruments. But Imperial's vacuum display graphics gave only instantaneous readings for time, date, elapsed time, fuel mileage, average and current speed, fuel level, miles per gallon, and range to empty.

sides, Chrysler had determined to transform its whole approach to building cars, and was intent on making the entire line front-wheel-drive at the earliest possible date. Deciding to give the Imperial the heave-ho after 1983 couldn't have taken the Board

No external changes were made for the 1982 model, but Kimberley cloth "mouse-fur" upholstery was new on the inside.

The factory says this is a 1983 model, but there is no way of telling since no changes were made. At only 1,407 units, this was the last and lowest production run of the three-year Imperial coupe.

of Directors more than five minutes, and it came and went in the 1990s with equal brevity. But I hope we'll see that name again.

Identification
1981: Unique (for Chrysler) bustle-back rear end, raked-back front end with Continental-like grille and hidden headlamps.

Specifications
Engines (net hp)
Type: cast-iron V-8
V-8, 318ci (3.91 x 3.31in), 140hp

Chassis and Drivetrain
Unit body and frame; shaft drive, four-wheel hydraulic brakes, steel wheels. TorqueFlite automatic transmission standard.

Size and Weight
Wheelbase (in): 112.7in
Curb Weight (lb): 1981 3,870lb; 1982 3,945lb; 1983 3,910lb

1982-83: No external changes; new Kimberley cloth (velvety) interiors in a choice of six colors accompanied the Mark Cross interiors among the no-cost buyer options.

Frank Sinatra (FS) Package: Special paint and emblems; a set of eight-track tapes with Sinatra's top hits housed in a special console.

Appraisal
Clearly some people consider the Imperial coupe worth acquiring. The rarity of the FS package, and never mind what I say about it, has to make it more desirable than standard jobs. Then again, if you preferred Bing Crosby . . .

Summary and Prospects
It's too early to discern any collector trends. The sheer scarcity of the car would suggest that fine examples will achieve some collectibility, and I suppose it's significant that it had stopped depreciating only five or six years after the last one rolled off the production line. Ordinary cars depreciate for about ten years when the more collectible ones start to turn around; those that are not collectible just keep depreciating.

Return on investment (95-point condition 1):

	1987	1995	*Return
	$6,000	$6,000	0.0%

*compound annual rate of return unadjusted for maintenance, insurance, and running costs

Production

	1981	1982	1983
Standard	7,077	2,050	1,427
FS Package	148	279	0

★★

Chapter 26

LeBaron Convertible
1982-95

The initial success of its survival-effort K-car convinced Chrysler Corporation to produce a variety of follow-up models using the same platform. Indeed for several years, critics would charge that all Chrysler offered was variations on the K. While this was essentially true, the variations were well-planned and timed to perfection—the basis of Chrysler's recovery in the 1980s. One such example was the convertible, which Lee Iacocca set out to revive after noting public reaction to a prototype he drove around Detroit. The prototype, like the production ragtops which followed, were built out of K-body coupes by a specialty firm, Cars and Concepts, Inc.

The Chrysler LeBaron convertible debuted along with its Dodge counterpart in 1982. It was the first Chrysler softtop since the 1970 Newport. The convertibles were making money by 1984 and had amortized their production costs. Dodge's version was dropped in 1986 but Chrysler's version shouldered profitably on.

A rakishly restyled LeBaron coupe was introduced in 1987 and the convertible version followed in the spring. Both were built on a different front-drive chassis than the LeBaron sedan and wagon, though the chassis dimensions were similar. Very fully equipped, these new convertibles came standard with rear window defogger, three-speed automatic transmission, automatic temperature control, power/heated outside mirrors, power door locks, two-tone paint, tilt steering wheel, cruise control, cassette player, power antenna, and dual map/courtesy lights mounted in the rearview mirror housing. This new convertible was wildly popular, and nearly 50,000 of the 1989 model were sold. The LeBaron was finally replaced by the new Sebring convertible in 1996.

What separates the second generation LeBaron ragtop from the first is clearly styling: the second generation has it, the first doesn't. That's not really fair: the 1982-86 cars were clean and efficient looking—but they'd hardly knock your socks off. The later cars look like 100mph standing still.

The most desirable LeBaron convertible from a driveability standpoint is the Mitsubishi V-6

Neatly turned out by Cars and Concepts in Detroit, the 1982 convertible was viewed by some as the answer to a question nobody asked, but turned out to be extremely popular. The best ones to acquire contain the Mark Cross leather interior and 2.6 liter engine.

version introduced starting in 1990. The V-6 provides refined power that is an improvement on the underwhelming baseline four-cylinder and the noisy turbos, although it won't perform with the latter.

LeBarons came standard with a manual transmission but most of them are found with the optional Torqueflite. Interiors were standard K-car, in the typical LeBaron style. Early models had the unfortunate, hard-to-read digi-graphic instrumentation and, for 1983-84, annoying "voice" warnings for everything from low oil pressure to "door ajar." The power top had a glass backlight and separate rear-quarter windows.

Special Models

Mark Cross package (1983-86) adds standard air conditioning, 2.6 liter Four, low-back Corinthian leather bucket seats with console and center armrest, leather-wrapped steering wheel, vinyl door

Another return for the Town & Country convertible, sort of: simulated white ash and mahogany body panels with the Mark Cross designer leather bucket seats, luggage rack, air, 2.6 engine, and other standard luxury equipment. It was almost exactly half the size and weight of the 1948 T&C on a about a foot-shorter wheelbase. The white car is a 1983, the darker one an '84.

And here are the same LeBarons in standard guise for 1983 (dark interior) and 1984.

trim inserts, Mark Cross identification, wire wheel covers, bumper guards, striping and cornering lights, Voice Alert, AM/FM, tilt-steering wheel, power windows and door locks, power deck lid, cruise control and Travel Computer.

Town & Country (1983-86): an additional package which applied pseudo wood trim to the Mark Cross convertible in the style of the old Chrysler Town & Country.

GT (1989-90): includes the 3.0 liter V-6, five-speed manual transmission, sport handling suspension, air conditioning, rear defogger, power door locks, heater, power mirrors, premium sound, leather-wrapped steering wheel, under-coating, and 205/60R15 high-performance tires on alloy wheels.

GTI (1989-94): includes the 2.2 liter intercooled Turbo IV PFI four-cylinder engine, HD transmission and brakes, performance suspension, illuminated entry, deck lid luggage rack, lighted visor mirrors, and 205/60R15 tires on alloy wheels. In 1990 the GTI adopted electronic variable damped suspension that allowed the driver to alter shock absorber damping.

Identification

1982-86: Standard LeBaron body trim with top-less body style.

1987-94: New, aerodynamic styling with hidden headlamps and small oblong grille.

Appraisal

The major driveability problem on first generation cars is cowl and body shake. The top works fine and Turbos are quick, yet reasonable on gas; handling is good and the size about right for four or maybe five passengers. Excess throttle lag and a lot of heat under the hood are typical problems for turbos. V-6 powered cars (1990-on) are smoother, far quieter, and for my money, a better buy. Most owners will disconnect the stentorian-toned vocal warning system on early models, a real piece of Mickey Mouse which lasted about as long as drivers took to listen to its repertoire. Parts and service are not a problem, and quality of fit and finish is very good. Second generation LeBarons look terrific, but their road manners aren't up to their styling and quality of fit and finish is mixed. A personal complaint I have about the 1987-94 models is that they don't really *feel* like convertibles; the windshield is raked so far back and the doors are so high that you feel encapsulated, without the airy sensation of the typical ragtop.

Summary and Prospects

There is no sign that these cars are going anywhere as investments, but the 1982-86 Town & Country will definitely be collectible in years to come through its casting-back to the days of the *real* T&Cs, which ended in 1950. Among the second generation cars, the GTC and, to a lesser extent the GT are more desirable for obvious reasons than the baseline or "Premium" or (later) the LX variations.

If the convertible body style again goes out of favor, all LeBarons will be in demand. Engine-wise, turbos and V-6s are the best bet. Sinking big bucks into one of these is not recommended, but don't buy a basket-case, either: they are complicated automobiles, and restorations are not cost-effective.

Price History

LeBaron convertibles are still depreciating, so there's no point in listing a price history. Current market values range between $3,000 and $4,500 for early examples, while the used car market determines the value of more recent examples. A factor presenting the late models from gaining in value soon is their sheer numbers.

The stylish second generation convertible, bearing the LeBaron name, was enormously popular, selling from 30,000 to 50,000 a year for six years. Illustrated is a monochromatic LeBaron GT coupe and convertible, mid-1989 model year specials with exterior moldings, die mirrors, wheels and grille all finished in white to match the body and interior.

Production

	1982	1983	1984	1985	1986
Standard	9,780	2,930	6,828	9,196	12,278
Mark Cross	0	5,441	8,275	6,684	6,905
Town & Country	0	1,520	1,105	595	501

	1987	1988	1989	1990	1991
Standard					
Mark Cross	8,900	41,568	49,119	38,962	35,296

	1992	1993	1994	1995
Standard				
Mark Cross	38,924	29,960	18,598	n/a

With intercooled turbo 2.2 and a handling suspension, the 1993 LeBaron GTC coupe is a capable road car but has, I suspect, low prospects for collectibility; however . . .

. . . the convertible GTC would be a better bet. This side view shows the radical windshield angle, which almost forms a glass roof over the front seat passengers and diminishes the open flavor. Still, a nice package, increasingly affordable as depreciation continues.

Specifications
Engines (net hp)
Type: overhead cam four
2.2 liters, 135ci (3.44 x 3.62in), 84-85hp standard 1982; 94-96hp standard 1983-84; 97-100hp standard 1985-88; 93hp standard 1989; 146hp (turbo) optional 1984-88; 174hp (turbo) optional 1989-94 (std GTC)
2.5 liters, 153ci (3.44 x 4.09in), 100hp optional 1986-87, standard 1988-94; 150-152hp (turbo) optional 1989-92
2.6 liters, 156ci (3.59 x 3.86in), 92-93hp optional 1982-85
Type: Overhead cam V-6
3.0 liters, 182ci (3.59 x 2.99in),141hp (standard 1990-95 Premium & GT, optional others)

Chassis and Drivetrain
Unibody construction.
Transmission: four-speed manual standard; Torqueflite automatic optional; five-speed manual optional starting in 1984
Suspension: MacPherson struts with coil springs and anti-sway bar front; beam axle, trailing-arms, coil springs and sway bars rear.

Size and Weight
Wheelbase (in): 1982-86 100.3in; 1987-94 100.6in
Curb Weight (lb): 1982-86 2,500-2,600lb; 1987-95 2,800-3,200lb

Chapter 27

Executive
1983-86

Another permutation on the ever-expandable K-car platform, this one was entirely unexpected: a long-wheelbase production Chrysler hadn't been on the scene since 1954 (although Imperial had preserved the breed on a semi-custom basis through 1965). Like the convertibles, these were conversions by a specialist builder, in this case ASC Corporation in St. Louis, hard by the Chrysler assembly plant. ASC stretched the K-body by adding 13in of wheelbase to the five-passenger sedan and 24in to the limousine, which gave it a 131in wheelbase: not as much as the old Crown Imperial, but long enough to provide extra-posh executive transport for seven. The limousine's rear area was upholstered in high quality cloth and the back seat was pillow-like with a center armrest; the front seats could be finished in cloth or leather and an divider window was standard on limousines. Chrysler called the Executive a combination of "traditional" limousine characteristics in a modern efficient size. At 210in long, it was huge for its time, with two rear-facing jump seats providing the extra passenger capacity but it was too narrow for limo use.

On paper these cars should have sold like hotcakes, and they did: 800 a year (1983 and 1984) is good going in the professional car trade and better than Imperial's long-wheelbase cars had ever done. It was a low profit margin, not sales, that finally did in the long-wheelbase K-cars.

Identification
1984: Straight K-car lines with extended wheelbase; only year for the sedan version.

A novel idea on paper, the K-car-based Executive limousine seemed to be the ideal vehicle for big city corporate users, but was not a profitable venture. Chrysler sold about 1,500 in three years. The limousine, on an extended, 131in wheelbase carried a division window which slides up behind the front seat, in the area blanked out by a thick "B" pillar. Extra passengers were accommodated by folding auxiliary seats.

The Executive five-passenger sedan rode a 124in wheelbase, the same size once used by the much less roomy New Yorker Brougham. Demand for this version was minimal and production lasted only a year.

1985: Limousine received new sound system with graphic equalizer, map pockets in front seatbacks, separate illuminated entry systems for the front and rear compartment, and a new 500-amp no-maintenance battery.

1986: Powered by turbocharged 2.2 liter instead of non-turbo 2.6. New deck lid panels and rear bumper fascia and endcaps were new.

Appraisal

These are quality products, painstakingly assembled by the specialist builder with a great deal of attention to interior quality and finish. They filled a certain need for compact yet roomy executive transport in their day, and many are still serving that role ten years later.

Summary and Prospects

No collector market has developed for these intriguing "professional Chryslers." They may have fallen into the psychological crack between the true limousines (wheelbases above 140in) and the plug-ordinary K-cars of the 1980s. I could not recommend these as investments any more than I could as collectibles. A handful have been saved as such, but they really represent the periphery of late model Chrysler collecting.

Price History

Price guides quote around $6,000 for examples in fine condition, a modest deprecation over the ten years since the last one was built (they sold originally at about $19,000 for the sedan and $22,000 to $27,500 for the limo). Nicely preserved ones will probably hold that value.

Specifications

Engines (net hp)
Type: overhead cam four
2.6 liters, 156ci (3.59 x 3.86in), 101hp (1984-85)
2.2 liters, 135ci (3.44 x 3.62in), 146 hp turbocharged (1986)

Chassis and Drivetrain
Unibody construction.
Transmission: TorqueFlite three-speed automatic.
Suspension: MacPherson struts with coil springs and anti-sway bar front; beam axle, trailing-arms, coil springs and sway bars rear.

Size and Weight
Wheelbase (in): 1983-86: 124in (sedan), 131in (limousine)
Curb Weight (lb): sedan 3,000lb; limousine 3,155lb

Production

	1983	1984	1985	1986
Sedan, 5pass.	n/a	196	0	0
Limousine, 7pass.	n/a	594	759	138

★

Chapter 28

Laser
1984-86

You'll have a good understanding of how Chrysler Corporation refined the Chrysler vs. Dodge image in the eighties by comparing their approach to two of their best packages, the K-body convertibles and the G-body sports coupes. The convertibles arrived in both Dodge and Chrysler guise in 1982, the sport coupes likewise in 1984 (Dodge Daytona and Chrysler Laser). By 1987, however, Chrysler had dropped the Laser and revamped the LeBaron convertible into a highly salesworthy package, while Dodge had dropped its convertible to concentrate on building Daytonas. The post-1986 LeBaron was a lot racier than its predecessor, but it was not in the sports car league of the Daytona.

The Laser initially outsold the Daytona, but by 1987 the Daytona was pulling away. The success of both the Chrysler LeBaron and Dodge Daytona after 1987 confirms Chrysler's canny decision to market a Dodge sport coupe and a Chrysler convertible.

Another derivation of the K-car platform, the G-24 sports coupe had a long lead time, during which prototypes amazed the automotive press with their "international" specifications. The Laser and Daytona had a much modified K-chassis featuring all-coil springs, front MacPherson struts, trailing arm rear beam axle and power rack-and-pinion steering topped by a husky 2+2 "fasthatch" body with design overtones of the Porsche 928. Introduced twelve years ago, they still look good today.

The Daytona was quickly accepted as a Dodge, with the performance pedigree for which that make is known, but the Laser was certainly an odd Chrysler. One of the smallest Chryslers in history, it came standard with manual transmission; instead of being aimed at Chrysler's traditional Buick-Olds rivals, it was targeted at the Pontiac Firebird and Datsun 280ZX; instead of aiming at the over-forty crowd, the Laser beamed its appeal at buyers under

With scores of aerodynamic sporty coupes flowing out of Detroit a decade later, it's hard to appreciate how exciting the Chrysler Laser was when it debuted in 1984. I parked one like this outside the General Motors Design Center in Warren, Michigan, just after it was announced; work stopped and a crowd gathered. Mr. Iacocca should have been there to see it.

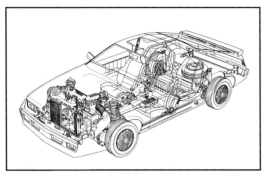

Phantom view of the Laser shows front-wheel-drive layout, 2.2 liter turbocharged engine, three-speed automatic, rack and pinion steering, bucket seats, hatchback storage area, and crash-preventing bumper systems. Five years earlier, nobody would have predicted this could have come from Chrysler Corporation.

thirty-five. It worked, though Chrysler had hoped for more than 50,000 sales a year.

The base model was powered by Chrysler's 2.2 liter four with throttle-body fuel injection. The premium Laser XE had a turbocharged 2.2 with port-type fuel injection and 142hp. The XE also featured

A stentorian male voice badgered the driver with mostly trivial information that the driver should have known about anyway. I'm surprised Congress didn't legislate something like this but even for them it would have taken things too far. Unpopularity quickly condemned the device.

The turbocharged, 145hp Laser XE was loaded with the latest electronics to include graphic instrumentation, navigator system, and stereo. A good five-speed manual transmission was a welcome option.

electronic instrument cluster, sports suspension, 15in tires, bucket seats with adjustable air bladders for thigh and lumbar support, on-board computer, and a twenty-two-function message center that gave visual and audible warnings of mechanical and operating failures.

The 1985 Laser was a mirror image of the '84, with minor alterations internally and a new raft of color selections. Gas-pressurized rear shocks were standard on all models, and those with sport suspensions also had gas pressurized front struts. An electronic wastegate control on the turbo 2.2 allowed higher maximum boost pressure and a slight increase in torque (168 up from 160 lb-ft.) Cast aluminum 15in wheels were now standard on the XE. In the Spring of 1985 a T-bar roof was introduced as an option with the sporty XT package (handling suspension, performance tires).

The final Laser in 1986 was slightly restyled with vinyl bodyside rub rails. A new engine choice was available in 1986: Chrysler's latest 2.5 liter four with throttle-body fuel injection, derived from the long-running 2.2. The added displacement came from an increase in stroke. The 2.5 also had two nodular iron balance shafts mounted between the crankshaft in the oil pan that helped reduce vibration, a frequent problem in large-displacement fours. It was standard in the Laser XE, optional in the base model. Engineering refinements included new cylinder heads for all three engines and a new, smaller distributor.

Identification

1984-85: The only external difference between the 1984 and 1985 Laser was their different colors. Trunk and fuel door remote releases are on center console.

1985: New adjustable seats with more lateral support; upshift indicator light for Lasers with five-speed gearbox; trunk and fuel door remote releases are moved to lefthand doorsill; soft-touch buttons for heating/ventilation system. Sporty XT model with removable roof panels, HD suspension, and P225/50R/15 tires added halfway through the model year.

1986: Bodyside moldings with vinyl inserts replace the ribbed moldings of 1984-85. Head restraints and intermittent rear window wiper were new features.

Appraisal

Even with the base suspension, Lasers are stable, predictable handling cars with excellent ride comfort given their size and short wheelbase. The base engine returns 0-60 in about 14 seconds, while the Turbo makes it just over eight. The driving position is low and sporty and the bucket seats are well shaped and supportive. The low seat, sloped tail, and thick roof pillars spoil the rear view; the manual shift linkage is rubbery and balky, so most owners may prefer the automatic. The XE and XT are the most desirable models, but ride quality suffers as handling is improved, so it's best to try one before you buy to see if you want to live with a stiff chassis.

Summary and Prospects

It is difficult to predict serious collectibility for the Laser, despite its many good qualities. One reason for caution is that it is really a fish out of water: a Chrysler in name but not in the Chrysler image, which the corporation itself recognized when it dropped the Laser in 1987 (although it was temporarily replaced by a Mitsubishi with a Chrysler badge). The Dodge Daytona has a much better (and longer) pedigree, and if investment is your prime consideration you'd be safer looking there. Still, the mint, low-mileage Laser will provide many happy driving hours, and it certainly doesn't cost an arm and a leg.

Price History

Lasers are still depreciating, so a price history is superfluous. Current used car market values models range between $1,500 and $3,000, but collectors pay up to $5,000 for extremely fine XEs and XTs.

Laser was little changed throughout its lifetime; this 1985 Turbo wears a new style of alloy wheels. On the inside were more buckety seats and more accessible hood/fuel door access.

Production

	1984	1985	1986
Laser	33,976	29,221	14,134
Laser XE	25,882	18,193	15,549
Laser XT	0	3,452	6,989

Specifications

Engines (net hp)
Type: overhead cam four
2.2 liters, 135ci (3.44 x 3.62 in), 97/99hp (std 1984-86)
2.2 liters, 135ci (3.44 x 3.62 in), 146hp turbo (std 1984 XE, opt other 1984s, opt 1985-86)
2.5 liters, 153ci (3.44 x 4.09 in), 100hp (std 1986 XE)

Chassis and Drivetrain
Unibody construction.
Transmission: four-speed or five-speed manual standard; Torqueflite automatic optional.
Suspension: MacPherson struts with coil springs and anti-sway bar front; trailing-arms with coil springs and sway bars rear.

Size and Weight
Wheelbase (in): 97.1in
Curb Weight (lb): 2,600-3,000lb

Chapter 29

Chrysler TC by Maserati 1989-91

An imaginative initiative, the TC ("Twin Cam") was designed to give Chrysler a rival to *luxus* coupes like the Cadillac Allante and Mercedes-Benz 560SL, but with a base price much lower: about $33,000. First known as the "Q-Coupe," it was built by Maserati using Chrysler componentry and the Italian maker's interior and body. Chrysler supplied the Dodge Daytona front-drive chassis (the K-car strikes again!), shortened to a 93in wheelbase and a length of only 176in: the smallest "Chrysler" ever. Power came from a double overhead camshaft version of the 2.2 liter Turbo packing 200hp; a 160hp single overhead cam Turbo was op-

tional. All TCs had a full-leather interior, a Maserati-tuned suspension, and four-wheel anti-lock disc brakes. The convertible top was manually operated but an electric motor pulled it taught when the top was up. When down, the top was stowed beneath a metal tonneau cover. A fiberglass removable hardtop with unnatural-looking opera windows was standard equipment.

As Chrysler had promised, the Mitsubishi-built overhead cam V-6 was made optional on the 1990 model (which didn't make it a "TC" anymore, but never mind); it was also the engine furnished when the buyer specified automatic transmission. The

With a 93in wheelbase, the smallest Chrysler ever built, the Maserati-influenced TC seemed like a good idea at the time. It was overpriced and overrated, and it didn't sell, but it certainly is a good per-forming LeBaron-variation, and at today's depreciated prices a clean one may be a better buy than they were new. Note Maserati trident emblem in center of grille.

Reminiscent of the two-seat Ford Thunderbirds, the lift-off hardtop was standard equipment on the Chrysler TC. Maserati trident is etched into the port-hole glass; tops were painted the body color.

The 1990-91 TCs carried a wreathed pentastar emblem instead of the Maserati trident, but were otherwise entirely unchanged. The best of these were bringing around $17,000 in mid-1995 but should have depreciated substantially by the time this book is published in 1996.

200hp dohc engine with five-speed remained the more sporty confection.

Chrysler called the TC a "beautiful little high-performance convertible with a designer label on it." Maserati is a manufacturer, not a designer, but even the improved '90 model was no competitor to Cadillac or Mercedes. Production was halted late in 1990 after just 7,300 were built, Chrysler having terminated the supply contact because of poor sales.

Identification

1989: LeBaron-like styling with unique grille: chrome surround, blacked out with a Maserati trident emblem centrally mounted.

1990: Unchanged in appearance. New driver's side airbag, woodgrain steering wheel, and V-6 engine available.

1991: No changes.

Appraisal

Unfortunately, upon introduction in January 1989, the TC was anything but a high-performance exotic. It looked all right, but withal not much different from the LeBaron convertible priced $8,000 less. It was fast, with precise steering, good brakes and handling, though the limp seats offered too little support and the clutch was heavy. The rest of it was pure K-car: lots of cowl shake and tacky dashboard controls, and buyers

of $30,000 cars don't expect that. Although Maserati had worked good things with the suspension, and though the engine "sings" above 3000rpm and delivers a real punch in the back, lots of more exciting looking convertibles could do that for a lot less money.

Summary and Prospects

The Chrysler-Maserati is depreciating rapidly; in the last two years the value of an average specimen has dropped by about 33 percent, and by 1996 even the dealers were retailing them for four figures. That would be the time to acquire the low mileage clean one, but acquisition ought to proceed in the clear knowledge that this is not what it tries to be. The magic name of Maserati is always worth something, but car for car the TC is less collectible than the LeBaron GTI, which at least is an honest car. The TC is an *ersatz* creation whose chief appeal is to people who don't know any better. That kind of automobile has never excited collectors, who are too sophisticated to be taken in.

Price History

Mint original low mileage (values from CPI price guide, Jan-March 93/95.

Chapter 30

Future Collectibles

The Chrysler LHS, the top of an exciting line of modern Chryslers, salutes tradition by wearing Walter Chrysler's old badge in the center of its grille. From the "B" pillar back this could be an XJ-series Jaguar. Roadability is about the same but the LHS is aerodynamically much superior and far more efficient fuel-wise. It also offers more space inside. It has what Jaguar used to advertise: "grace, space and pace."

Silhouette and cockpit of the Chrysler Concorde, which shares its platform with the LHS but has more conventional styling. Cab-forward design allows a cavernous interior, and this purposeful dashboard is marred only by the obviously fake wood trim above the glovebox and around on the door fillets.

Latest and greatest: the 1996 Chrysler Sebring, lineal successor to the LeBaron convertible and a better car in every way, offers the collectors of 2050 something to wax nostalgic over; they'll probably be looking for those mint originals.

Index